for C   GROWERS

Frédéric Thériault
and
Daniel Brisebois

A *COG* Practical Skills Handbook

Canadian Organic Growers
Cultivons biologique Canada

Crop Planning
for organic vegetable growers
First published in 2010

Canadian Organic Growers Inc.
323 Chapel Street · Ottawa
Ontario · K1N 7Z2 · Canada
Tel.: 613-216-0741   Fax: 613-236-0743
www.cog.ca   publications@cog.ca

Production
Editor:
  Sheila Globus
Design and Layout:
  Jean-Michel Komarnicki, JMK Image-ination
Cover design:
  Won Pyun
Front cover photograph:
  Everdale Organic Farm & Environmental
  Learning Centre
Back cover photograph:
  Laura Berman, GreenFuse Photos
Project Manager:
  Kristine Swaren, Blue Chicory Communications

Library and Archives Canada Cataloguing in Publication

Thériault, Frédéric
  Crop planning for vegetable growers : COG practical skills handbook / Frédéric Thériault, Daniel Brisebois.
  Includes bibliographical references.
  ISBN 978-0-9808987-1-2
  1. Vegetable gardening--Canada--Handbooks, manuals, etc.
  2. Farm management--Canada--Handbooks, manuals, etc.
  I. Brisebois, Daniel, 1977–
  II. Title.
SSB323.C3T45 2010   635   C2009-907491-5

Printed and bound in Canada

Canadian Organic Growers
Cultivons biologique Canada

CHANGES IN THE ORGANIC SECTOR have been dramatic since COG's inception in 1975. A movement then struggling to be noticed is now a multi-million dollar industry with widespread consumer recognition and national standards backed by federal regulation.

Organic agriculture is now the fastest growing sector in agriculture, and as such it is the most economically and environmentally viable solution for Canada's rural areas.

COG has a significant positive impact on organic growing in Canada through our policy and media work, educational materials, production statistics, scholarships, farmer training, market development, and the grassroots work of our fifteen regional chapters.

ORGANIC AGRICULTURE:

- sequesters carbon in the soil and produces food with energy efficient methods
- increases soil organic matter and a diversity of living soil organisms
- improves water quality and quantity
- improves biodiversity
- improves the health of soil, plants, animals, farm workers, consumers
- increases farm financial viability by reducing dependence on inputs and providing farmers a fairer return for their products

---

COG is a federally registered charity (no. 13014 0494 RR0001). Our members are farmers, gardeners, processors, retailers, researchers and consumers who share a vision of a sustainable bioregionally-based organic food system.

COG's MISSION is to lead local and national communities towards sustainable organic stewardship of land, food and fibre while respecting nature, upholding social justice and protecting natural resources.

JOIN CANADIAN ORGANIC GROWERS
OUR NATURE IS ORGANIC

CONTENTS

ACKNOWLEDGMENTS

THIS HANDBOOK grew out of the crop planning experience we gained working on farms where we apprenticed and worked. Daniel would like to thank his farm mentors Lorenz Eppinger, Ken and Martha Laing, and especially Alison Hackney who entrusted him with her crop planning. Frédéric would like to thank Stephen Homer on whose farm he had his first opportunity to do crop planning and where he learned to love agriculture, its rewards, and its challenges.

Collectively, the techniques we learned were further developed at la Ferme Coopérative Tourne-Sol and for that we owe sincere thanks to Reid Allaway, Renée Primeau and Emily Board. We'd also like to thank Becky Lipton for her part in starting the farm.

The growers we interviewed provided us with a range of perspectives and planning styles that served to challenge and flesh out our own. Thanks to Maude-Hélène Desroches (QC), Frédéric Duhamel (QC), Robin Turner (ON), Heather Stretch (BC), Bree Eagle (BC), Dan Wiens (MB), Wally Satzewich (SK), Norbert Kungl (NS), Ken and Martha Laing (ON), Hilary Moore(ON), Maureen Bostock (ON) and Ann Slater (ON).

Thanks also to those who reviewed the manuscript at various stages in the writing process and provided their encouragement and feedback: Danielle Chevalier, Jean-Martin Fortier, David Merson, Michelle Jory, Harris Ivens and Leslie Moskovits. And thanks to Sheila Globus and Kristine Swaren who edited the book.

Finally, thank you to Dana Chevalier and Emily Board for their constant support and love.

Daniel Brisebois and Frédéric Thériault
January 2010

THIS HANDBOOK was funded in part by Agriculture and Agri-Food Canada through the Advancing Canadian Agriculture and Agri-Food (ACAAF) program. We wish to acknowledge the support of the following organizations for making this publication possible: the Investment Agriculture Foundation of British Columbia, the Manitoba Rural Adaptation Council, the New Brunswick Agriculture Council / Conseil Agricole Nouveau-Brunswick, the Territorial Farmers Association and the Yukon Agricultural Association.

Agriculture and Agri-Food Canada (AAFC) is pleased to participate in the publication of this guide. AAFC is committed to working with its industry partners to increase public awareness of the importance of the agriculture and agri-food industry to Canada. Opinions expressed in this handbook are not necessarily those of AAFC.

THE AUTHORS

Frédéric Thériault started as an apprentice in 2001, working up to crop manager of the same farm three years later. He has a B.Sc. in Plant Sciences with minors in Agricultural Economics and Ecological Agriculture, and has a M.Sc. in Agriculture and Environment. He taught Ecological Agriculture and Principles of Plant Sciences at McGill University. He is part of Équiterre's CSA steering committee.

Daniel Brisebois started farming in 2000. He has worked both as an apprentice and field manager on different farms. Daniel has a B.Sc in Agricultural Engineering. He is on the steering committee of the Eastern Canadian Seed Growers Network and is Vice-President of Canadian Organic Growers.

Frédéric Thériault and Daniel Brisebois

Frédéric and Daniel are two of the founding members of la Ferme Coopérative Tourne-Sol in Les Cèdres, Quebec. Founded in the fall of 2004, Tourne-Sol now produces certified organic vegetables, flowers, seeds, seedlings and herbal teas on 12 acres rented from an organic grain farm. Tourne-Sol sells through a 250-share CSA, a farmers market, and an online seed catalogue.

    Daniel and Frédéric are also active members of le "Réseau des Jeunes Maraîchers Écologiques" – a group of young Quebec farmers who meet regularly to share experience and resources.

INTRODUCTION

THIS BOOK TACKLES A BIG TOPIC – CROP PLANNING. What exactly is crop planning? Crop planning is a process for figuring out which crops you want to grow, when to plant them, and in what quantities. This is best done before you actually have to do it in the field.

The crop planning process described in this book was developed over a number of years on different farms where we have worked. It has served us well at Tourne-Sol cooperative farm. To make it relevant to other farmers, we spent a lot of time talking to several growers about how they plan their crops. Not everyone's crop planning processes were as mathematical and as detailed as ours. But the overarching principles were the same for all the successful farmers we spoke with: set objectives for the season, figure out roughly how much to grow, order the seeds, take some notes during the growing season, and use those notes to plan the following year.

This practical skills handbook presents a detailed 11-step crop planning approach. In steps 1 and 2, you will set financial goals for your crop plan and then determine how to meet them through your marketing outlets. In steps 3 to 8, you will develop the actual crop plan. Your crop plan will consist of a 3-ring binder containing a field planting schedule, field maps, greenhouse schedule, seed order and field operations calendar. In step 9, you will learn how to implement your crop plan and record what actually happens. In steps 10 and 11, you will analyze how your crop plan succeeded and start your planning for next year.

This process is useful for vegetable growers regardless of their level of experience or size of their operation. Its methods apply not only to commercial growers, but also to homesteaders. We recommend that newer growers pay close attention to steps 1 through 7. Experienced farmers who have already built a solid crop plan will gain most from step 4 and steps 8 through 11. These steps go beyond simple crop planning and look at how your crop plan fits into your long-term vision for your farm.

The book also presents the profiles of eleven vegetable growers from across the country. They showcase a range of operations from a small intensive acreage that works with walking tractors and hand tools to large farms that rely on cultivating tractors and sizeable workforces. They are all examples of how good crop planning helps a farm thrive.

The appendices at the end of the book contain important information. Appendix A presents three vegetable reference charts you'll need when completing most of the book's worksheets. Refer to them regularly. Appendix B outlines an additional step that needs to be taken the first year you crop plan but not in subsequent years. Have a look at appendix B before you jump into step 4. Other appendices contain complementary information, charts and references.

So put down your hoes and harvest knives, pick up your pens and calculators and let's get crop planning!

ACCESS TO FORMS

All the forms used in this book can be downloaded from the COG website www.cog.ca in two formats :

- pdf to photocopy for paper-based systems
- spreadsheet (MS Excel) with formulas included, for computer-based systems

SOME THOUGHTS ABOUT MEASUREMENT

The standard units of measurement in Canada are metric, but most growers we meet use imperial units. In fact, on our farm, we generally talk in terms of feet and inches.

All reference charts present data in both metric and imperial, and all formulae can be used with either. Worksheets, schedules and examples in the text are in imperial, but you will find the same charts with metric measurements in Appendix D. Whichever you use, it is important that you stay consistent through your planning.

Here are a few conversions that will come in handy:

- 1 meter = 3.38 feet
- 1 ft = 0.3 m
- 1 acre = roughly 208 ft * 208 ft = 43,560 sq ft
- 1 ha = 100 m * 100 m = 10,000 m^2
- 1 ha = 2.47 acres
- 1 kg = 2.2 lbs
- 1 lb = 0.454 kg

MEET BRUCE AND HANNA

Bruce and Hanna, a fictional couple, are embarking on a career growing vegetables. The 11 crop-planning steps in this handbook will follow their decision-making process as they flesh out their farm vision and crop plan.

Bruce and Hanna met while they were apprentices on a farm with a 200-share CSA and farmers market stand. They enjoyed the experience and returned for the next two years to learn more. Now they feel confident they could start a farm and manage their own business.

After looking for a few months, they found 1.5 acres to rent, split on two adjacent lots. They then borrowed a small amount of money to buy equipment. For their first years, they will use their own personal vehicle, a hatchback, as their delivery vehicle and will charge their mileage to the farm business.

BRUCE AND HANNA'S INITIAL INFRASTRUCTURE INVESTMENT

ITEM	COST
Cold Room	$1,800
Irrigation System	$1,500
Walking Tractor with Rototiller	$3,500
Seeder	$200
Handtools	$500
Total	$7,500

All costs provided in the book are examples only and may not reflect your costs.

1 SET YOUR FINANCIAL GOALS

Effective crop planning doesn't begin with crops, but with your pocket book. You have to know how much money you want or need to make in order to figure out how much to seed. Step 1 presents a three-part approach to holistic financial planning; it will guide you in your budget design and will offer a simplified approach for beginners. When you have completed this step, you should have a budget that shows your gross sales target, your salary target and a rough draft of your expenses for the upcoming year.

HOLISTIC FINANCIAL PLANNING

Allan Savory of the Center for Holistic Management[1] developed a three-part approach to holistic financial planning which we have simplified a little. He recommends to start by planning the **income**, then the **profit** and finally, the **expenses**. For us this will mean begin by planning your gross sales, then determine your retained earnings (salary) and finally plan the expenses.

Some profitable farms spend 25% of their gross sales on expenses, others spend 75%. It all depends on the size of their operation and on whether they hire help. Each case is unique. Be sure to set a gross sales target that suits your circumstances and that you can achieve with careful budgeting. Prioritize and limit expenses to save a larger portion of your gross sales for yourself. This process makes the difference between a profitable farm and one that loses money. After all, *one dollar saved is like two dollars earned.*

PLAN YOUR FARM INCOME

How many dollars worth of vegetables can you produce and sell a year? That's the first question to ask yourself as you set your **gross sales target.** If you have been farming for a while, you can realistically estimate the vegetables you are able to grow and how much money you can make from them. If you are a new grower, this question might leave you perplexed. Your capacity to produce

1. Savory, Allan & Butterfield, Jody, 1999, *Holistic Management: A New Framework for Decision Making.* Island Press

depends on several things, but foremost on your vegetable growing experience.

Anne Weil, agronomist with Club Bio-Action in Quebec, has noticed that independent of scale, the gross income per hour of the top diversified vegetable growers in Quebec is relatively constant. They average $18 per hour each person (owner or employee) works.

In general, a farm owner works about 2,000 hours in a year. This would produce $36,000 of **gross** revenue (before expenses) and sets the upper limit you can expect to make if your farming system runs almost perfectly. One full-time beginner can likely produce $5,000-$10,000 of gross sales. Keep these numbers in mind as you determine a **gross sales target** for your farm.

PLAN YOUR SALARY

How much money do you need to earn this year? What are your living and personal expenses? How much do you want to set aside in savings? Consider whether you will be earning off-farm income.

It's helpful to sketch a personal budget but personal expenses should not be mingled with business expenses. In the business numbers, your personal financial needs are all lumped into one line item—the **salary** or **retained earnings** line.

Choose the salary that you want to draw from your farming business next year. If several partners manage the farm, choose a total salary amount for all of the farmers. Remember, you won't get rich farming. You will enjoy a pleasant, simple lifestyle, not an extravagant one.

PLAN YOUR EXPENSES

Subtract your retained earnings (salary) from your farm income (gross sales target). The amount that remains is what you have available to cover this year's expenses.

If you have records of expenses from previous years, start with those. Look at every expenditure category and the amounts spent. Determine how much you will need to spend this year. Try to reduce expenses where possible. Spend your money where it will give the best return and provide the greatest benefit for your farm system.

If you are starting up and don't have past numbers to work with, get sample budgets from other growers, farmer's organizations, or conferences. Make sure the numbers you use are from a similar-sized farm as the one you are planning. Or, to create your own budget, call suppliers for the prices of the inputs you'll need.

Save your receipts and keep track of your expenditures. (For computer users, several financial software applications are available to ease the process.) Be sure not to exceed the amount budgeted for your expenses. If you do, try to compensate by reducing other budget items. At times, this may feel frustrating, but at the end of the year, you will be happy if you can pay yourself what you planned to – and maybe even get a bonus!

Financial planning for first-time farmers

Even if you don't know what things cost or how much your farm can make, you can still estimate what you need to grow. Simply change the order of the 3-point planning approach:

- **Plan your salary.** Determine your salary or retained earnings target.
- **Plan your farm income.** Multiply your salary by 2. This is your **gross sales** target. Consult other farmers to make sure it is realistic.
- **Plan your expenses.** Use the other half of your gross sales and allocate it to the various expense categories in your budget.

Should you rent or buy land to farm?

Renting land

Renting reduces start-up expenses. As a new famer, low rent payments will give you financial breathing room to establish a business and acquire tools. If you buy land later, you will have a clearer idea of what to look for.

Owning land

Buying land offers longterm stability and helps build equity as you invest in soil amendments and infrastructure, but it is more costly. It will likely put more strain on your cash flow, and may reduce your profit margins.

Remember, if your farm is also your home, separate the portion of your mortgage payments that is a business expense (cultivated fields and buildings) from your personal expense (house, woodlot, extra land, etc.) to get a more accurate idea of your farm finances. This will also help you compare your numbers to what is suggested here.

Table 1.1 shows a budget summary for Bruce and Hanna, as well as a budget example for a 38-share CSA[2]. (See appendix E for a detailed version of Bruce and Hanna's budget.)

Use these as guidelines to draft a start-up budget. Remember every farm is different. These examples don't replace careful research and budgeting.

Here is how Bruce and Hanna set their financial targets with the simplified approach:

- **Plan the salary:** *They do not want to work off-farm during the growing season, but will work off-farm during the winter. In their first year, Bruce and Hanna each want to make $5,500 from the farm. Their combined **salary target** is $11,000.*
- **Plan the farm income:** *Their gross sales target is: $11,000 * 2 = $22,000 Their 3 years of farming experience tells them this is an ambitious, but reasonable, production goal.*
- **Plan the expenses:** *Table 1.1 shows their budget.*

Ferne Coopérative Tourne-Sol

Farmers market display

2. Equiterre. 2006. 4 *Modèles économiques viable et enviables d'ASC*. Equiterre. http://www.equiterre.org/agriculture/informer.php

Gross sales: the starting point for your crop plan

Whether you use the simplified or the standard approach, once you've completed this step you should have:

- A **gross sales target** based on your capacity to produce. (This is the starting point for your marketing plan in step 2)
- A **salary target** based on your personal financial needs
- A **budget** for your business expenses

TABLE 1.1: SAMPLE BUDGET FOR A START-UP FARM

	BRUCE & HANNA		ÉQUITERRE 38 SHARES	
	$	%	$	%
INCOME	$22,000	100%	$19,010	100%
CSA Baskets	$12,000		$19,010	
Farmers Market	$10,000			
EXPENSES	$10,835	49%	13,272	70%
Fixed Costs				
Administration	$1,490	7%	$2,090	11%
Insurance	$500	2%	$0	0%
Land and buildings	$1,900	9%	$1,686	9%
Financial and Other	$1,270	6%	$5,156	27%
Operating Expense				
Supplies	$1,650	8%	$1,783	9%
Greenhouse	$1,250	6%	$0	0%
Field Operations	$725	3%	$531	3%
Marketing	$650	3%	$398	2%
Vehicle	$800	4%	$1,330	7%
Other	$600	3%	$298	2%
RETAINED EARNINGS FOR FARMER	$11,000	50%	$5,120	27%
NET FARM INCOME	$165	1%	$618	3%
= Income – (Expenses + Retained earnings)				

All costs provided in the book are examples only and may not reflect yours.

LES JARDINS DE LA GRELINETTE
MAUDE-HÉLÈNE DESROCHES AND JEAN-MARTIN FORTIER, ST-ARMAND, QUEBEC

FROST FREE:
mid May to late
September

FARM SIZE:
7 acres, 1.5 acres in
vegetables

MARKETING:
100 CSA shares,
farmers market,
wholesale mesclun
mix

LES JARDINS DE LA GRELINETTE is well known across Quebec as an example of a successful small acreage farm. Maude-Hélène and Jean-Martin were among the 2008 nominees for Quebec's young farmer business contest, *Tournez-vous vers l'excellence.*

After four years of farming on rented land in New Mexico and Quebec, Maude-Hélène and Jean-Martin founded *Les Jardins de la Grelinette* in 2005 in the Eastern Townships. They describe their operation as a micro-farm. With vision and planning, they have grown the business to a size ideally suited to the available growing space and desired sales targets.

Both work on the farm full time with the help of 2 to 4 apprentices or volunteers. They gross about $100,000 on an intensively managed 0.8 hectare (1.5 acres). Sales are split between a 100 member CSA (65%), a farmers market (25%), and wholesale mesclun (10%) sold to local grocery stores and restaurants.

To control costs, Maude-Hélène and Jean-Martin farm bio-intensively with very little machinery. Soil is prepared and tilled with a BCS walking tractor and various attachments. Inexpensive manual tools help with seeding and weeding.

Most root crops, lettuces and greens are double-cropped. Cucurbits, Solanaceae and Brassicas are single cropped, and are preceded or followed by a cover crop.

To prepare their 4' x 100' beds they
- destroy the cover crop with the BCS flail mower
- incorporate the cover crop with the BCS rototiller
- apply compost and incorporate with a BCS rotary plow or rototiller

Tunnels and greenhouses are used to grow Solanaceaes, Cucurbits, early and late salad mixes, and celery. They have two 16' x 100' unheated tunnels and two 24' x 100' structures with minimal heat.

Maude-Hélène and Jean-Martin organize their records in a large binder, alphabetically by crop. They record varieties and quantities as well as seeding, transplanting, and harvesting dates. They also keep track of any treatments or operations performed on the crop.

Since their current crop plan meets their marketing objectives, their annual crop planning consists mainly of tweaking last year's seeding dates and quantities. They have a set rotation with specific blocks dedicated to each crop family. Within these blocks, the individual crops are juggled. They include trials to explore for reliable organic varieties.

Jean-Martin and Maude-Hélène have found it easy to meet their summer market and CSA needs with abundant Solanacea, Cucurbit, and bean production, so they focus their attention on the first and last weeks of the season when fewer crops are available.

Their main planning tool is a large calendar on which they write dates and quantities to seed in the field and greenhouse. They also list other key crop-management tasks. "We are slaves to our production calendar," says Maude-Hélène. "We put the calendar together, then there are no further questions. We just follow it."

LES JARDINS DE LA GRELINETTE
MAUDE-HÉLÈNE DESROCHES AND JEAN-MARTIN FORTIER, ST-ARMAND, QUEBEC

2 DEVELOP A MARKETING PLAN

IN THE PREVIOUS STEP, you set a target for the gross sales you would like to make with the vegetables you grow. How are you going to sell those vegetables? And what quantities will allow you to meet your gross sales target? Answer these questions with a simple marketing plan that takes into account the following:

- Distribution methods
- Product list
- Price
- Weekly sales projections
- Weekly harvest targets

DISTRIBUTION METHODS

There are many ways to sell vegetables: farm kiosk, restaurant orders, Community Supported Agriculture (CSA), farmer's markets, bulk orders, Internet orders, and health food stores, for example. There is room for local farmers in all of these markets.

Choose distribution methods that match your preferences, your contacts, your competition and the market demand. In the beginning, limit yourself to one or two marketing outlets; each outlet takes time to develop and manage.

FARMERS MARKETS AND ON-FARM KIOSKS

Farmers markets and **on-farm kiosks** are simple. You harvest what you think you can sell, bring it to your stall and wait for customers. It may be difficult at first to predict how much you'll sell but eventually you'll get a sense of how much people will buy. Often you'll find you end up selling similar amounts from one week to the next.

RESTAURANT OR GROCERY STORE SALES AND WHOLESALE ORDERS

Restaurant or grocery store sales and **wholesale orders** add a step: you send your client a list of what you have available and then harvest exactly what they want. In some cases, these clients can estimate what they will need from you before the season starts.

COMMUNITY SUPPORTED AGRICULTURE (CSA)

Community Supported Agriculture (CSA) is a way for customers to share the risks and benefits inherent in farming. Customers purchase a share of the harvest ahead of time and receive a weekly basket of vegetables throughout the summer. The content of the basket varies seasonally and with availability. CSAs have seen tremendous growth in the past 20 years.

DIFFERENCES BETWEEN CSA AND OTHER TYPES OF MARKETS

CSA

- Basket content changes from week to week
- Need to harvest a quantity equal to your total number of shares for all vegetables in a given week; except if choices between items are allowed in the basket.

- Harvest needs are easy to predict before season
- A base of staple crops is needed

- 20–30 crops have to be grown at all times even though only 9–13 crops are harvested each week
- A set number of weeks of commitment

OTHER DIRECT MARKETING

- Market offerings should stay constant every week
- Different quantities of each crop can be harvested; Quantities change from week to week with weather and holidays–just a few items can be sold if most crops are unavailable

- Harvest needs are hard to predict before season
- A focus on specific vegetable niches or on a broad range is possible

- Could choose to specialize in 5 – 10 crops or grow over 40. It depends on your market
- Commitment can be variable depending on the market

Decide how much of your **Gross Sales Target** (step 1) will come from each marketing outlet.

Since Bruce and Hanna have worked on a farm that did both CSA and farmers market, they decide to do the same. It's what they know best. They would like to focus mainly on CSA but are afraid of being committed to too many clients in their first year. They split their gross sales between the two outlets and aim to make $12,000 from their CSA, and $10,000 from the farmers market .

PRODUCT LIST

Next, you will need to decide which vegetables to sell. Think about what you like to produce, the kind of work you like to do, and the equipment and facilities available to you.

Once you have your niche, create your product list. This shows all the vegetables you intend to grow and sell. Decide how you'll sell each vegetable – as a bunch, per kg, or by the head, for example.

KNOW YOUR NICHE

Consider specializing in one of these niches:

- vegetables that are staples of people's diets
- specific crops such as garlic or salad greens
- specialty items such as coloured carrots or radishes
- food items for ethnic markets
- items for chefs and haute cuisine
- bulk quantities such as fall roots or crops for canning or freezing

---

PRICES

Choose a price for each product on your list. If you have several formats or sizes for one item, determine the price for each of them and write it on your product list.

At first, your prices will depend on the market prices and on your own perception of what vegetables are worth. Visit the produce section in the grocery store and check the prices. Do the same at local farmers markets. Get a feel for what other people are charging. Some farmer associations provide sample price lists. Do not limit yourself to these prices though. If your produce is organic, fresher, tastier, and more colourful, it can command a higher price.

Later, you will be able to adapt your price list to reflect crop profitability. Step 10 explores the relationship between pricing and the space or harvest time that crops require.

COMMUNITY SUPPORTED AGRICULTURE (CSA) PRICES

- **Decide how long your CSA will run.** In Canada, CSAs typically start in mid-June and run 16–22 weeks until the end of October. You can start earlier or end later, but it takes solid planning, storage facilities and plenty of experience. If you are new to CSA, start with a shorter commitment.
- **Decide what a weekly share of vegetables will be worth.** A weekly value of $15 to $30 is typical. The more expensive the share, the more vegetables you will need. If you offer two different share sizes, simplify planning by making the large share twice the size of the small share.
- **Set a share price.** Multiply the weekly share value by the number of weeks your CSA will run; add other charges such as delivery or administrative costs. That's your share price.

Bruce and Hanna hope to earn $12, 000 from their CSA.
- *The season will run 16 weeks. This gives them the flexibility to delay the first pickup weeks if the spring proves to be difficult.*
- *They aim for a price of $22/week.*
- *Each share will cost $352 (16 weeks * $22/week)*
- *They decide to sell 35 shares (35 shares * $352/share = $12, 320).*

SALES PROJECTIONS

Now that you have sales targets for each outlet and a product list with prices, you can make your sales projections. A sales projection sheet is a visual representation of what you plan to sell each week – and therefore what you need to grow. It can also be used to estimate how much money you'll make on a weekly basis.

FOR EACH MARKETING OUTLET:

- Start with a blank *sales projection* template
- Label the sheet to identify the marketing outlet it corresponds to
- List the **crops** you want to sell during the season along with their prices
- List all the weeks you will be at a particular outlet. Use the Monday date regardless of the actual delivery day to make it easier to combine all your sales sheets later
- In each **date** column, enter the quantity of each item you think you can sell that week

- Enter the total volume of sales for each vegetable in the **total units** column
- Multiply the **total units** by the **price**, and enter it in the **total $** column
- Add all the values in the **total $** column. This is the amount you can expect to make at that outlet if your sale projections are accurate
- Adjust your numbers so the sum of the **Total $** column falls within a 10–15% range above your **sales target** for the outlet

To simplify wholesale and market sale planning, use a consistent quantity each week. For example, if you think 20 bunches of carrots will sell at market, enter 20 for each week of harvest on your sales projection sheet. If you think chefs will order 40 heads of lettuces a week, enter 40 each week.

FILL OUT A SALES PROJECTION SHEET FOR YOUR CSA:

CSA sales projection sheets are a little different. You will create a sales projection sheet for a single share, and later multiply the results by the number of shares you intend to sell.

- Start with a blank *sales projection* template; label it *CSA basket contents*.
- Fill out the **crop, price and units** columns, as well as the **dates,** just as you did for the previous sales projection sheets.
- For each **date,** set the quantity of units of each vegetable for the share. Refer to CHART A3 to see what is in season, and add a new item each week to maintain diversity. Remember to keep a supply of staple vegetables that everyone likes and recognizes.
- At the bottom, calculate the total share value for each week and compare this to your target share value.
- Adjust the share contents to have 10% to 15% more than the planned weekly goal.

*Bruce and Hanna make a **CSA sales projection sheet** (table 2.1). They plan for a share value of $23 to $26 per week to make sure they can meet their $22 weekly average. If crops are abundant, the CSA shares might be bigger than expected, or the extras could be sold at the farmer's market.*

*They also make a **market sales projections sheet** (table 2.2), with the same list of vegetables as the CSA. Since their space is limited, they want to focus on vegetables that are more profitable per growing area and decide not to grow potatoes, broccoli or beans for market. If there is a surplus of these crops that the CSA can't handle, they will bring them to market. However, they do plan on growing peas for market as they will have less to offer at that time of year.*

TABLE 2.1: CSA SALES PROJECTION:
WEEKLY CONTENT OF BRUCE AND HANNA'S SHARES

CROP	$ VALUE	UNIT	02-JUL	09-JUL	16-JUL	23-JUL	30-JUL	06-AUG	13-AUG	20-AUG
Arugula	$2.50	bunch	1	1						
Basil	$2.50	bunch			1				1	
Beans	$3.00	lb			2	2	1	1	1	1
Beets	$2.50	bunch		1	1		1			1
Broccoli	$2.50	head	1	1	1	1	1	1	1	
Carrots	$2.50	bunch			1	1	1	1	1	1
Cilantro	$2.00	bunch	1			1				
Cucumbers	$0.75	fruit				3	3	3	3	3
Garlic	$1.50	head					1	1	1	
Kale	$2.50	bunch	1	1						
Kohlrabi	$1.50	head	2	1	1					
Lettuce	$2.00	head	1	1	1	1	1	1	1	1
Onions	$1.50	lb				2	2	2	2	2
Parsley	$2.00	bunch		1			1			1
Peas	$5.50	lb	2	2						
Peppers	$1.00	fruit							2	2
Potatoes	$1.50	lb								
Radish	$2.00	bunch	1	1	1					
Scallions	$2.00	bunch	1	1	1	1				
Squash, summer	$0.75	fruit			3	3	3	3	3	3
Tomatoes	$2.00	lb						2	2	2
WEEKLY SHARE VALUE* IN $			$23.50	$24.50	$25.75	$24.50	$23.50	$25.50	$25.00	$25.50

* Weekly Share value is calculated by pricing each item in the basket and adding up the total.

All prices provided in the book are examples and may not reflect prices in your markets.

CROP	27-AUG	3-SEP	10-SEP	17-SEP	24-SEP	1-OCT	8-OCT	15-OCT	TOTAL UNITS
Arugula					1	1	1		5
Basil	1			1					4
Beans	1	1	1	1					12
Beets	1	1				1	1	1	9
Broccoli					1	1	1	1	11
Carrots	1	1	1	1	1	1	1	1	14
Cilantro		1			1		1		5
Cucumbers	3	3	3						24
Garlic	1		1	2	2	2		2	13
Kale						1	1	1	6
Kohlrabi					1	1	1		7
Lettuce	1	1	1	1	1	1	1	1	16
Onions			2	2	2	2	2	2	22
Parsley			1			1		1	6
Peas									4
Peppers	2	2	2	2					12
Potatoes		2		2	2		2	2	10
Radish									3
Scallions									4
Squash, summer	3	3	3						27
Tomatoes	2	2	2	2					14
WEEKLY SHARE VALUE	$24.50	$25.50	$24.50	$25.00	$24.50	$24.00	$24.00	$23.00	

TABLE 2.2: MARKET SALES PROJECTIONS FOR BRUCE AND HANNA

CROP	$ VALUE	UNIT	02-JUL	09-JUL	16-JUL	23-JUL	30-JUL	06-AUG	13-AUG	20-AUG
Arugula	$2.50	bunch	15	15	15	15	15	15	15	15
Basil	$2.50	bunch			10	10	10	10	10	10
Beans	$3.00	lb								
Beets	$2.50	bunch		20	20	20	20	20	20	20
Broccoli	$2.50	head								
Carrots	$2.50	bunch			40	40	40	40	40	40
Cilantro	$2.00	bunch	15	15	15	15	15	15	15	15
Cucumbers	$0.75	fruit				75	75	75	75	75
Garlic	$1.50	head					50	50	50	50
Kale	$2.50	bunch	10	10	10	10	10	10	10	10
Kohlrabi	$1.50	head	15	15	15	15	15	15	15	15
Lettuce	$2.00	head	40	40	40	40	40	40	40	40
Onions	$1.50	lb				40	40	40	40	40
Parsley	$2.00	bunch		10	10	10	10	10	10	10
Peas	$5.50	lb	17.5	17.5						
Peppers	$1.00	fruit					30	30	30	30
Potatoes	$1.50	lb								
Radish	$2.00	bunch	20	20	20					
Scallions	$2.00	bunch	15	15	15	15				
Squash, summer	$0.75	fruit			60	60	60	60	60	60
Tomatoes	$2.00	lb						80	80	80
WEEKLY MARKET VALUE* IN $			$458	$528	$505	$581	$656	$816	$816	$816

* Weekly Market value is calculated by pricing each item and adding up the total.

All prices provided in the book are examples and may not reflect prices in your markets.

CROP	27-AUG	3-SEP	10-SEP	17-SEP	24-SEP	1-OCT	8-OCT	15-OCT	22-OCT	TOTAL UNITS	TOTAL $
Arugula	15	15	15	15	15	15	15	15		240	$600
Basil	10	10	10	10						100	$250
Beans										0	$0
Beets	20	20	20	20	20	20	20	20	20	320	$800
Broccoli										0	$0
Carrots	40	40	40	40	40	40	40	40	40	600	$1,500
Cilantro	15	15	15	15	15	15	15	15	15	255	$510
Cucumbers	75	75	75	75	75					750	$563
Garlic	50	50	50	50	50	50	50	50	50	650	$975
Kale	10	10	10	10	10	10	10	10	10	170	$425
Kohlrabi	15	15	15	15	15	15	15	15	15	255	$383
Lettuce	40	40	40	40	40	40	40	40		640	$1,280
Onions	40	40	40	40	40	40	40	40	40	560	$840
Parsley	10	10	10	10	10	10	10	10	10	160	$320
Peas										35	$385
Peppers	30	30	30	30						240	$240
Potatoes										0	$0
Radish						20	20	20	20	140	$280
Scallions										60	$120
Squash, summer	60	60	60	60	60					660	$495
Tomatoes	80	80	80	80	80					640	$1,280
	$816	$816	$816	$816	$761	$540	$540	$540	$423		$11,245

Turn your sales projections into harvest targets

Before you can sell your vegetables, you have to harvest them. To convert your sales projections into your harvest targets, combine the projected sales sheets that you completed for each of your marketing outlets into a single sheet.

- Start with a blank *sales projection* template and label it *Harvest Targets*
- List all the **crops** and **prices**
- Enter the first date of each week of sales at any marketing outlet.
- For each vegetable, add the quantities for each date on each sales projec-

TABLE 2.3: BRUCE AND HANNA'S HARVEST TARGETS

Crop	Unit	02-Jul	09-Jul	16-Jul	23-Jul	30-Jul	06-Aug	13-Aug	20-Aug
Arugula	bunch	50	50	15	15	15	15	15	15
Basil	bunch	0	0	45	10	10	45	10	10
Beans	lb	0	0	70	70	35	35	35	35
Beets	bunch	0	55	55	20	55	20	20	55
Broccoli	head	35	35	35	35	35	35	35	0
Carrots	bunch	0	0	75	75	75	75	75	75
Cilantro	bunch	50	15	15	50	15	15	15	15
Cucumbers	fruit	0	0	0	180	180	180	180	180
Garlic	head	0	0	0	0	85	85	85	50
Kale	bunch	45	45	10	10	10	10	10	10
Kohlrabi	head	85	50	50	15	15	15	15	15
Lettuce	head	75	75	75	75	75	75	75	75
Onions	lb	0	0	0	110	110	110	110	110
Parsley	bunch	0	45	10	10	45	10	10	45
Peas	lb	70	70	0	0	0	0	0	0
Peppers	fruit	0	0	0	0	30	30	100	100
Potatoes	lb	0	0	0	0	0	0	0	0
Radish	bunch	55	55	55	0	0	0	0	0
Scallions	bunch	50	50	50	50	0	0	0	0
Squash, summer	fruit	0	0	165	165	165	165	165	165
Tomatoes	lb	0	0	0	0	0	150	150	150

tion sheet. Enter this amount for the appropriate **harvest date**. (To combine CSA shares with other outlets, multiply each CSA item by the total share number before adding it).

Your *harvest targets worksheet* shows how much of each vegetable you need to harvest every week through the season. This is the starting point for your crop plan. In step 3 we will determine how much and when to plant to meet these targets.

Table 2.3 shows Bruce and Hanna's harvest targets. To add CSA projections to market projections they first multiply each CSA item quantity by 35 shares.

CROP	27-AUG	3-SEP	10-SEP	17-SEP	24-SEP	01-OCT	08-OCT	15-OCT	22-OCT	TOTAL UNITS
Arugula	15	15	15	15	50	50	50	15	0	415
Basil	45	10	10	45	0	0	0	0	0	240
Beans	35	35	35	35	0	0	0	0	0	420
Beets	55	55	20	20	20	55	55	55	20	635
Broccoli	0	0	0	0	35	35	35	35	0	385
Carrots	75	75	75	75	75	75	75	75	40	1090
Cilantro	15	50	15	15	50	15	50	15	15	430
Cucumbers	180	180	180	75	75	0	0	0	0	1590
Garlic	85	50	85	120	120	120	50	120	50	1105
Kale	10	10	10	10	45	45	45	45	10	380
Kohlrabi	15	15	15	15	50	50	50	15	15	500
Lettuce	75	75	75	75	75	75	75	75	0	1200
Onions	40	40	110	110	110	110	110	110	40	1330
Parsley	10	10	45	10	10	45	10	45	10	370
Peas	0	0	0	0	0	0	0	0	0	140
Peppers	100	100	100	100	0	0	0	0	0	660
Potatoes	0	70	0	70	70	0	70	70	0	350
Radish	0	0	0	0	0	20	20	20	20	245
Scallions	0	0	0	0	0	0	0	0	0	200
Squash, summer	165	165	165	60	60	0	0	0	0	1605
Tomatoes	150	150	150	150	80	0	0	0	0	1130

Teamwork Farm
Hilary Moore, Lanark, Ontario

Frost free:
late May to late September

Farm size:
2 acres in vegetables

Marketing:
67 CSA shares, restaurant and store

Hilary Moore of Teamwork Farm grows vegetables on two acres using draft horses. She sells 80% of her vegetables through a 67 share CSA, and the rest to restaurants and health food stores.

Crop planning at Teamwork Farm starts with a detailed budget that includes annual (recurring) and durable (capital) expenses plus her personal salary. The total budget figure becomes her gross sales target, which is divided by the CSA share price to determine how many shares she will need. She then decides on the makeup of each share and calculates how much of each crop she needs to grow. Hilary converts sales to other outlets into a certain number of CSA shares in order to include them in the harvest targets. This is all done using computer spreadsheets.

Planting dates are determined with a Biodynamic calendar. Hilary photocopies each calendar page of the growing season and tapes the "notes" portion of the copy on top of the corresponding original. On the top copy, she writes her to-do list by date – planting and cultivation activities. On the original underneath, she tracks what actually happened when.

Besides sales targets, Hilary also considers available labour and the land that is ready for growing. The harvest needs are converted into a field plan and seed order. She advises, "It's helpful to deliberately underestimate yields and overestimate seed requirements. If the weather cooperates and there's a great harvest, you can always offer specials to your customers."

Ferme Coopérative Tourne-Sol

CSA drop off

3 MAKE FIELD PLANTING SCHEDULES

Y OUR FIELD PLANTING SCHEDULE is a summary of the crops you plan to grow, when to plant them, and how much of each to plant. It is the first part of your crop plan. To create one, you will convert your harvest targets (step 2) into field dates and bed lengths using one worksheet for every crop in your marketing plan. You will then consolidate all your worksheets into a preliminary schedule.

FIELD WORKSHEET

Growing spaces are often expressed as an area in sq. ft or m². We have chosen to use bed lengths instead (bed meters or bed feet). A bed length is the linear portion used of a growing bed.

We work with bed length rather than row length. This will make it easier in step 4 to compare and manipulate the number of beds to optimize field layout.

For each crop, take a blank field worksheet template; label it with the crop's name. On the worksheet, work backwards from your harvest dates and harvest needs to determine field planting dates (field dates) and how much to plant (bed length). Note that these worksheets deal with crops and not with varieties. You will only consider specific vegetable varieties in step 5.

Notice that there are 2 columns for "field date" and 3 columns for "bed length" in the worksheet. Field dates and bed lengths are first calculated mathematically on a week-by-week basis. Then, you have to make some judgment calls based on your farm management practices to determine actual field dates. Group your actual bed lengths according to these actual field dates.

Use information from step 2 and appendix A to fill out each column as follows:

Harvest Date:
Transfer your **harvest dates** (from your **harvest targets** worksheet from step 2) into the rows of the first column. Each row corresponds to a different harvest week.

TABLE 3.1: BRUCE AND HANNA'S LETTUCE FIELD WORKSHEET

HARVEST DATE	DTM	FIELD DATE		HARVEST NEED HEADS	YIELD	ROWS PER BED	FIELD SF	BED LENGTH		
		CALCULATE FIELD DATE	ACTUAL FIELD DATE					CALCULATE PER WEEK	CALCULATE PER PLANTING	ACTUAL PER PLANTING
				HEADS	HEADS PER FT			BEDFT	BEDFT	BEDFT
03-JUL	35	29-MAY	22-MAY	75	1	3	1.3	32.5	32.5	35
10-JUL	35	05-JUN	05-JUN	75	1	3	1.3	32.5	65	65
17-JUL	35	12-JUN	05-JUN	75	1	3	1.3	32.5		
24-JUL	35	19-JUN	19-JUN	75	1	3	1.3	32.5	32.5	35
31-JUL	35	26-JUN	26-JUN	75	1	3	1.3	32.5	32.5	35
07-AUG	35	03-JUL	03-JUL	75	1	3	1.3	32.5	32.5	35
14-AUG	35	10-JUL	10-JUL	75	1	3	1.3	32.5	32.5	35
21-AUG	35	17-JUL	17-JUL	75	1	3	1.3	32.5	32.5	35
28-AUG	35	24-JUL	24-JUL	75	1	3	1.3	32.5	32.5	35
03-SEP	35	31-JUL	31-JUL	75	1	3	1.3	32.5	65	35
10-SEP	35	07-AUG	31-JUL	75	1	3	1.3	32.5		
17-SEP	35	14-AUG	14-AUG	75	1	3	1.3	32.5		
24-SEP	35	21-AUG	14-AUG	75	1	3	1.3	32.5		
01-OCT	35	28-AUG	14-AUG	75	1	3	1.3	32.5	162.5	165
08-OCT	35	03-SEP	14-AUG	75	1	3	1.3	32.5		
15-OCT	35	10-SEP	14-AUG	75	1	3	1.3	32.5		
22-OCT	35	17-SEP		0	1	3	1.3	0		

DTM (Days to maturity):

Enter the DTM from CHART A1 or A2. This is the number of days a crop takes from planting in the field until it is ready for harvest. The DTM ratings in the charts represent the earliest standard varieties on the market. DTM is affected by weather, sunlight, and variety choice. These factors will be taken into account when you choose your planting frequencies and varieties.

Field date:

Field date is short for *field planting date*. To keep all your worksheets synchronized, always use the first day of a week as a field date. Field date will be first mathematically calculated, but you will later revise your actual field dates based on your chosen planting frequency.

SYNCHRONIZE FIELD DATES

The **planting frequency** column in CHARTS A1 and A2 indicates how often to plant a crop to maintain a steady supply of fresh produce.

- **Some vegetables need only be planted once in the season.** The same plants are harvested repeatedly through the season (tomatoes) or can be stored to sell over an extended period (onions, celery root).
- **Other crops need to be regularly planted to maintain a fresh constant supply.** If planted too infrequently these plants may become bitter or woody (lettuce, kohlrabi), grow too big (beets, carrots), or succumb to disease that reduces yields (cucumbers, summer squash).

Getting set up to plant takes time. Try to plant as much as you can while you have your seeding and transplanting equipment in the field.

- Schedule planting on Mondays. If the weather doesn't cooperate you can switch planting with other tasks scheduled for later in the week, such as greenhouse seeding or office work.
- Set your first possible **field date** when the ground thaws and drains in spring.
- Schedule field dates every 2 weeks. Succession crops can be planned for every 2 weeks or every 4 weeks depending on how they hold in the field.

- Determine if you'll need weekly plantings of temperamental crops like radishes or brassica greens, which generally grow very quickly, or lettuce which grows quickly in the summer heat.
- Check whether frost dates will affect the planting frequency of any of the crops planted only once.

Bruce and Hanna's neighbours tell them that in most years they can work their soil as of May 1 and that their last frost is usually around May 20. They decide to spend the first week of May preparing the soil and to start planting their frost-hardy crops May 8.

Starting May 8, they'll plant every 2 weeks. The subsequent **field dates** will be May 22, June 5, June 19, and so on. They will add frost-sensitive plants to the schedule beginning May 22.

Exceptions to this schedule:

- Peas: plant as soon as possible. Peas thrive in cool weather.
- Tomatoes: wait one week after the frost date to make sure frost doesn't nip plants.
- Lettuce: In the heat of the summer (June 19 to July 31), plant them every week.

Calculated Field Date:

[Harvest Date - DTM = Field Date]

- Using a calendar, start with your harvest date and count back the number of days to maturity to find your first field date. For each subsequent week simply enter the following week's date in the field date column.
- Check CHART A3 to be sure that the **field date** isn't earlier than the crop can be planted, in which case you would have to revise your harvest targets (step 2)

Actual Field Date:
- Consult the "Synchronize Field Dates" sidebar to choose your planting frequency and synchronize the field dates on all your crop worksheets.
- Write down the dates in the actual field date column that correspond to your synchronized field dates. These are the dates you actually plan on planting in the field.
- Consult CHART A3 to verify the latest date each crop can be planted. This should be the last date in the actual field date column. Do not rely too much on your final plantings until you have a few years of experience with whether they are adequate.

Harvest Target:
For each harvest date, enter the harvest target from step 2.

Yield:
Enter the crop **yield** from CHART A1 or A2. Make sure the units are the same as those of your harvest needs. Crop yield is the total amount harvested from an area over the whole season. For some crops it's the entire plant, for others it's the quantity of fruit or leaves picked over many weeks. The values in CHART A1 and A2 are conservative recommendations. Over time you can generate your own list of yields (step 11). Note that if your yield is in row feet your bed length (below) will be in bed feet (bedft). If your yield is in row meters your bed length will be in bed meters.

Rows/Bed:
Enter the recommended number of rows per bed from CHART A1 or A2, subject to the considerations presented in the Field Layout section in Appendix B.

Field Safety Factor (Field SF):
This value is a multiplication factor that will increase the bed length grown to ensure you will meet your harvest targets. It allows you to offset potential field losses. Enter 1.3 as your **field SF**. Step 11 addresses how to make changes to the field SF as you gain experience.

Bed Length:
This is the amount of linear bed space (bedft or bedm) a crop will require in the field. Calculate the bed length for each harvest week, group them by actual field date and round off.

- **Calculate bed length per harvest week**

  [{(harvest needs ÷ yield) ÷ rows/bed} * field SF = Bed length/harvest week]
- **Calculate bed length per planting**

  For each actual field date enter the sum of all the associated Bed length/ harvest week. Make sure you only write it once.
- **Actual bed length per planting**

  Round off the bed length calculated per planting. Aim for full beds or whole fractions of the beds set in the Field Layout section in Appendix B. When rounding down, consider the impact it will have on your safety factor.

Bruce and Hanna first calculate the lettuce bed length they need each week:

- *Calculated bed length per week*

  *[{(75 heads ÷ 1 heads/rowft) ÷ 3 rows/bed} * 1.3 = 32.5 bedft of lettuce/harvest week]*
- *Calculated bed length per planting*

  On June 5, they will be planting lettuce for 2 harvest weeks (July 10 and 17). They add the bedft for these two harvest weeks and obtain 65 bedft to be planted on June 5. July 31 is similar. On August 14, the last possible planting date for lettuce, they will be planting for 5 harvest weeks. They add the required bedft and obtain 162.5.

  > *Note that lettuce is Bruce and Hanna's only crop that deviates from the biweekly planting schedule. Between June 19 and July 31 they will plant weekly, and will need 32.5 bedft each week.*
- *Actual bed length per planting*

  They round off 32.5 bedft per planting date to 35 bedft and leave 65 bedft as is.

Trellised pole peas

Ferme Coopérative Tourne-Sol

Make field planting schedules

PRELIMINARY FIELD PLANTING SCHEDULE

Once your field worksheets are completed, organize them by family and incorporate them into a planting schedule.

Start a blank *field planting schedule template.*

■ Fill out the **Field Date** columns across the top with the Monday of each week you will be planting in the field. (This should correspond to the field dates on all your worksheets)

■ Complete each row and column:
  » Enter the **Crop**
  » Enter the **Family** in the notes column.
  » Enter the **rows/bed** and the **inrow spacing**.
  » Transfer the **actual bed length** you intend to plant on each **field date**.
  » Add all the bed lengths together to determine the **Total Bed Length** you will plant during the season
  » Divide the **Total Bed Length** by the full length of your bed (from your *field layout*) and enter the result in the **Total full beds** column.
  » Skip one row between crop families.

You have now completed a fundamental piece of your crop plan. Your *preliminary field planting schedule* shows how much of each crop you need to plant and when to plant it in order to satisfy your harvest needs and marketing plan. Steps 4 and 5 will flesh out this schedule according to your field layout and variety choices.

CROPS PLANTED ONCE IN THE SEASON

You don't need a worksheet for crops you plant only once. Instead:

- *Determine your first harvest date (make sure you are not expecting to harvest any crops before this date)*
- *Calculate your bed length [{(Harvest needs ÷ yield) ÷ rows /bed} * field SF = bed length]*
- *Round off if necessary*

Bruce and Hanna's harvest goals from their marketing plan: 1,130 lbs of tomatoes over the whole season.

- *Rows/Bed: 1*
- *Yield: 2.2 lbs/ row ft*
- *Field SF: 1.3*
- *Calculate the bed length: [{(1130 lbs ÷ 2.2 lbs/ row ft) ÷ 1 row/bed} * 1.3 = 668 bedft]*
- *Round off:*

Bruce and Hanna decide to plant 700 bedft, which is seven 100 ft long beds.

TABLE 3.2: PART OF BRUCE AND HANNA'S PRELIMINARY FIELD PLANTING SCHEDULE

CROP	NOTES	ROWS PER BED	INROW SPACING	FIELD PLANTING DATE					
				01-MAY	08-MAY	22-MAY	05-JUN	19-JUN	26-JUN
Garlic	Allium	3	0.5 ft						
Onions	Allium	3	1 ft		400				
Scallions	Allium	3	0.5 ft		50				
Arugula	Brassica	3	DS				50	20	
Broccoli	Brassica	3	1 ft		65	65	65	65	
Kale	Brassica	3	1 ft			35		15	
Kohlrabi	Brassica	3	1 ft				65	35	
Radish	Brassica	3	DS				50	35	
Lettuce	Aster	3	1 ft			35	65	35	35
Beets	Chenopod	3	DS		130		130		
Basil	Labiatea	3	1 ft			25	25	15	
Beans	Legumes	2	DS			200	100	100	
Peas	Legumes	1	DS	500					
Carrots	Umbel	3	DS		130		260		
Cilantro	Umbel	3	DS			25	15	35	
Parsley	Umbel	3	1 ft		35		35		
Cucumbers	Cucurbits	1	DS			200		200	
Squash, summer	Cucurbits	1	DS			100		100	
Peppers	Solanacea	2	1.5 ft				200		
Potatoes	Solanacea	1	DS			200			
Tomatoes	Solanacea	1	1.5 ft				700		
				ALL BED LENGTHS IN BEDFT					

DS : Direct Seeded, a crop that is seeded directly in the field as opposed to transplanted.

The spacing between the plants (inrow spacing) is determined by the adjustment of the seeder.

FIELD PLANTING DATE									TOTAL BED LENGTH	STANDARD BED LENGTH	TOTAL BEDS
03-JUL	10-JUL	17-JUL	24-JUL	31-JUL	14-AUG	28-AUG	11-SEP	16-OCT			
								300	300	100	3
									400	100	4
									50	100	0.5
15		15		15	20	50	35		220	100	2.2
				130					390	100	3.9
		15			50				115	100	1.15
35		35		35	100				305	100	3.05
						50			135	100	1.35
35	35	35	35	65	165				540	100	5.4
100		130		100					590	100	5.9
25		25							115	100	1.15
100		100							600	100	6
									500	100	5
260				330					980	100	9.8
15		15							105	100	1.05
50									120	100	1.2
		100							500	100	5
		100							300	100	3
									200	100	2
									200	100	2
									700	100	7
ALL BED LENGTHS IN BEDFT											

SELWOOD GREEN
NORBERT KUNGL, BRAMBER, NOVA SCOTIA

FROST FREE:
mid-May to late
October

FARM SIZE:
30 acres in
vegetables

MARKETING:
3 markets, green
grocers, health
food stores and
restaurants

NORBERT STARTED FARMING AT SELWOOD GREEN, near the Minas Basin, in 1986. He grows organic vegetables on 30 acres with 10 seasonally full time employees, and a few more during peak season.

Norbert's main fields are divided into groups of four blocks. Each block contains five 6' x 200' beds and corresponds to a different step in his crop rotation:
- Year 1 High fertility crops and greens
- Year 2 Medium fertility crops and greens
- Year 3 Low fertility crops
- Year 4 Cover crops

One of Norbert's markets is 52 weeks a year. His growing season is extended in three 24' x 96' greenhouses, which provide winter spinach and red Russian kale. In the summer, he grows tomatoes and English cucumbers in the covered space. The greenhouses are only heated when cucumbers are planted in the ground, and when seedlings are started.

He cautions new farmers not to grow too many early crops unless they have a guaranteed good return for them. Early planted crops usually have high weed pressure, and need costly inputs such as perforated plastic or floating row cover.

Norbert uses a mathematical planning method similar to the one presented in this handbook. He begins with his harvest needs and works backwards to create a seed order.

On a single master sheet:
- each line represents a different crop
- each detail column represents a client or market
- cell values are the weekly harvest needs for each client by crop
- totals columns show the total harvest needs, planting quantity (calculated from the harvest needs), and planting dates

Planting dates are planned by crop: lettuce is planted every week and cole crops every 2 weeks. Carrots and beets have 2 to 3 plantings for bunching plus large plantings in early July for storage crops.

The amount to plant on each date is adjusted to compensate for slower growth in the spring and fall. For example, the last lettuce plantings grow slower but hold well in the field; Norbert plants 50% more than normal for a couple of weeks and then 100% more for the last two plantings.

The final planting quantities and dates are then transferred to a notebook. For each week, Norbert uses the right-hand page to make a to-do list; on the left, he records what actually happens. The to-do list is compiled in the following sequence:

- planting quantities are transcribed to the appropriate weeks
- weeks are counted backwards to determine when to start transplanted crops in the greenhouse; the number of trays to seed each week is noted

Seed needs are calculated based on the total amount of trays or beds to be planted for each crop.

The master sheet shows 115 vegetables listed according to how they are marketed. Rather than simply enter "lettuce," Norbert lists distinct types, such as green leaf lettuce, red leaf lettuce and romaine. Similarly, summer squash is distinguished as green zucchini, yellow zucchini, and patty pans. Norbert grows multiple varieties for each of these categories to adapt to climatic conditions.

Norbert always reads seed catalogue descriptions to find promising new varieties. He focuses his trials on crops that are important to his farm and on those crops for which he is not satisfied with the current varieties. He limits trials in the summer however, because he finds it hard to keep track of them.

Norbert tries to take a few days after Christmas to do planning. Although it can be difficult fitting it into his schedule Norbert makes this winter task a priority. "The better you prepare your cropping season on paper," he says, "the easier it is not to forget anything during the summer."

4 CREATE CROP MAPS

Y OUR FIELD PLANTING SCHEDULE tells you **how much** to plant and **when** to plant it. The crop maps you'll create in this step will show you **where**. Start by putting your crops into blocks, keeping in mind your planting schedules and any crop rotation considerations. Then, balance crop bed lengths to make sure beds and blocks are full. From your balanced block planting schedule, create a crop map for each block. Finally arrange your field blocks into a crop rotation.

CROP ROTATION CONSIDERATIONS

A crop rotation is the general plan of how crops move and succeed one another in the field over many years. A good crop rotation will help an organic farmer break his or her dependence on crop protection chemicals, reduce weed pressure, improve soil fertility, and even reduce the workload. Crop rotations have important long-term benefits and are thus a crucial aspect of the organic management of a farm. They are also required for organic certification.

The following four considerations will help you decide which crops to grow together:

Pests and Disease

Crops that are susceptible to the same pests and diseases should be grown together. Pests and diseases are usually specific to crop families. Some families such as *Cucurbitaceae*, *Solanaceae* and *Brassicaceae* are more prone to attack than others and benefit most from a long crop rotation.

Field dates

Field management tasks are easier to accomplish when co-ordinated in a single large area with multiple beds, as opposed to many areas where single beds are planted. Put crops planted on the same field date together in the same block if you can, in order to create as large a field area as possible. This allows for more comfortable manoeuvring during ground preparation, cover crop seeding and compost spreading. It also lets you irrigate a larger area at once, use wider pieces of row cover for season extension or insect control, and focus your weeding energies on recently planted crops.

Harvest Time

Group crops with close harvest dates together. It will be easier to cover crop the large bare area that's left after harvest. Some suggested groupings include: crops such as radishes and salad greens that cycle through the garden in 4–5 weeks, beets and fresh carrots (7–9 weeks), and leeks, celeriac and storage carrots (11+ weeks).

Fertility requirements

Group crops according to their fertility requirements. This lets you fertilize a whole area with the same application rate. Crops can be classified as heavy feeders (Brassicas, Solanaceaes, Cucurbits, Alliums), medium feeders (certain root crops, leafy vegetables) and light feeders (root crops, beans and peas).[1]

Crop field blocks

The *field layout* instructions (in Appendix B) tell how to divide your fields into modular field blocks. This needs to be done before continuing with step 4.

Field blocks are the units of your crop rotation. You will now decide which crops will go into which blocks, keeping the previous crop rotation considerations in mind. This involves three steps:

- Grouping crops into blocks with roughly the same number of beds
- Making a preliminary planting schedule for each block
- Balancing the schedule by adjusting the bed lengths

GROUP CROPS INTO BLOCKS

The figures in the total full bed column on your *preliminary field planting schedule* (step 3) indicate how many beds each crop fills over the season. Use these figures to place crops into blocks.

Start with one of your more pest and disease sensitive families (Solanaceae, Brassicaceae and Cucurbitaceae for most farms):

- Add up the **total full beds** for each crop in the family.
- Compare the number of beds required for this family with the number of beds in one of your blocks.
- See whether you can pair this family with other crops with similar rotation considerations (field dates, harvest dates or fertility requirements) to complete the block.

1 Gagnon, Yves. 2003. *La Culture Écologique Pour Petites et Grandes Surfaces.* 3^{ieme} édition révisée. Les Éditions Colloïdales.

Proceed this way for each of your pest- or disease-sensitive families. Once you have built blocks around these families, assign the remaining crops to other blocks.

HOW MANY BLOCKS HAVE YOU JUST CREATED?

If you build more blocks than you have in your field layout you can do one of the following:

- Assign more crops for the same blocks with the intention of double cropping
- Adjust your harvest needs in step 2 to choose crops that offer a better profit-to-available-planting-space ratio
- Consider preparing more land to grow on (this does come with additional costs, work load, and maybe even travel time)

If you build fewer blocks than you have in your field layout, use the extra blocks to:

- Plant crops that don't fit in other blocks as you make your **balanced block planting schedules.**
- Plant cover crops for the whole year. It may seem costly to not use all your land for growing vegetables, but cover crops will improve your soil structure, add fertility, and reduce weed pressure for future years.

Bruce and Hanna's blocks have 15 beds, each with a full bed length of 100 feet. These are the 6 blocks they came up with:
They have 3 Blocks based around the most disease and pest sensitive crops:
- ***Solanacea:*** *they need 11 beds in their plan. They add 3 garlic beds. Garlic is planted in the fall and overwintered. They will plant the garlic in the fall before the Solanacea crops will be planted. This leaves one bed empty to complete as they balance the contents of each field block.*
- ***Cucurbits:*** *8 beds. Cucurbits are planted 3 times in the season and are heavy feeders. Bruce and Hanna don't want to put any crop in this block that is planted more often. They pair the 4 beds of onions and 0.5 bed of scallions with the cucurbits. Alliums will do well with a high rate of fertilization. They leave this block with 12.5 beds until later in the planning.*
- ***Brassica:*** *11.7 beds. They pair these with cilantro and parsley. Brassica crops are planted every 2 weeks. Bruce decided he should pair the Brassicas with a crop that would also be planted regularly. He decided to go with cilantro and parsley. Both these crops have small bed fractions planted every 2 weeks.*

It will be easy to combine these crops in such a way that beds get completed on every planting date. This brings him pretty close to his 15 beds in the block. He will adjust these numbers when he balances his blocks. Bruce also looked at the fertility needs while making this choice. Though Brassicas are considered heavy feeders while parsley and cilantro aren't, the latter are not negatively affected by too much fertility.

Bruce and Hanna also have 2 blocks of mixed crops totalling 33.5 beds. All of these crops are planted frequently during the season and are medium or light feeders. They will either place the surplus beds in other blocks or crop the same area twice in the season (double cropping).

One additional block remains. They will keep it in cover crops for the full season. When Bruce and Hanna balance their blocks, they will not use this block for excess crops.

PRELIMINARY BLOCK PLANTING SCHEDULE

Now you know which crops to plant together in each field block. Transfer the information from your preliminary planting schedule so that each block has its own planting schedule. The total bed length in each block may be different from the actual growing area that's available. Ideally, you want them to be the same. Here's what to do: look at the total bed length for each planting date. If the bed length doesn't correspond to a whole number of beds, set a target length that does. Then compare that target length to the available growing space.

- For each block take one *planting schedule template; label it **Preliminary Block Planting Schedule***
  - » Transfer the information from the preliminary planting schedule to the appropriate block planting schedule.
  - » Add three additional rows labelled **Total Bed Length, Target Bed Length** and **Target Full Beds**
- For each **planting date** column:
  - » Add the bed lengths for each of the crops and enter the **Total bed length**. This is the bed length to plant on a particular date.
  - » In the **target bed length** row, round the total bed length up or down so that it is a full bed or a logical fraction.
  - » Calculate the number of **target full beds**
    [Target bed length ÷ full bed length = target full beds]

Add the **target full beds** values. Enter the total in the **Total Full Beds** column. Compare this value with the number of beds in your block.

- If it is less, put the block aside and return to it later.
- If you have more beds than you have space for, consider one of these options:
  » Reduce your target bed lengths for the block
  » Try to find a place for these excess beds in other blocks
  » Double crop some of your beds in this block or in another block

Table 4.1 shows Bruce and Hanna's preliminary field schedule for their mixed blocks.
- *The **May 1** planting is easy to deal with: 500 bedft is equal to five 100 ft beds.*
- *The **May 8** planting calls for 260 bedft. They round this up to 300 bedft, which is equal to 3 beds.*
- *On June 26, July 10 and July 24 Bruce and Hanna only have 35 bedft of lettuce scheduled. This number is too low to round up. They use these lengths to complete either the planting from the week before or the week after each of those dates.*

TABLE 4.1: PRELIMINARY BLOCK PLANTING SCHEDULE

Crop	FIELD PLANTING DATE												TOTAL BED LENGTH	STANDARD BED LENGTH	TOTAL FULL BEDS
	01-MAY	08-MAY	22-MAY	05-JUN	19-JUN	26-JUN	03-JUL	10-JUL	17-JUL	24-JUL	31-JUL	14-AUG			
Lettuce			35	65	35	35	35	35	35	35	65	165	540	100	5.4
Beets		130		130			100		130		100		590	100	5.9
Basil			25	25	15		25		25				115	100	1.15
Beans			200	100	100		100		100				600	100	6
Peas	500												500	100	5
Carrots		130		260			260				330		980	100	9.8
TOTAL Bed length	500	260	260	580	150	35	520	35	290	35	495	165	3,325	100	33.25
Target bed length	500	300	300	600	165	35	565	35	300	35	465	200	3,500	100	35
Target full beds	5	3	3	6	1.7	0.3	5.7	0.3	3	0.3	4.7	2			35
ALL BED LENGTHS IN BEDFT															

DOUBLE CROPPING

Planting two crops in the same year is called double cropping; planting three crops is called triple cropping. Quick-growing crops such as spinach, lettuce, or radishes, can easily be doubled or triple cropped. Fall planted garlic can be planted after a previous crop has been harvested.

If you plan on double cropping, the previous crop has to be harvested and the residue has to be incorporated before the next one can be planted. You might also need to spread more compost to ensure adequate fertility for the second crop.

BALANCED BLOCK PLANTING SCHEDULE

You have identified a target bed length for every planting date. Now modify the bed length of each crop so that the total bed length planted each date equals the target bed length. We call this "balancing field blocks".

- For each block, take one planting schedule template; label it ***Balanced Block Planting Schedule.*** As you transfer the information from the preliminary block planting schedule to the balanced block planting schedule, revise the bed lengths so that they add up to your **Target bed length.**
- When all the numbers in the **Total bed length** row equal those in the **Target bed length** row, you are finished balancing your block.
- After you've balanced your blocks, fill any partially-filled or empty beds with additional vegetables. These are backups in case of crop failures. If you don't need the crop till it in as a cover crop.

TABLE 4.2 : BALANCED BLOCK PLANTING SCHEDULE

CROP	FIELD PLANTING DATE												TOTAL BED LENGTH	STANDARD BED LENGTH	TOTAL FULL BEDS
	01-MAY	08-MAY	22-MAY	05-JUN	19-JUN	26-JUN	03-JUL	10-JUL	17-JUL	24-JUL	31-JUL	14-AUG			
Lettuce			35	65	35	35	35	35	35	35	65	200	575	100	5.75
Beets		150		135			100		135		100		620	100	6.2
Basil			35	35	30		30		30				160	100	1.6
Beans			230	100	100		100		100				630	100	6.3
Peas	500												500	100	5
Carrots		150		265			300				300		1,015	100	10.15
TOTAL Bed length	500	300	300	600	165	35	565	35	300	35	465	200	3,500	100	35
	ALL BED LENGTHS IN BEDFT														

After balancing all of their blocks, Bruce and Hanna were left with one empty bed in the solanacea and garlic block. They decided to cover crop this bed for the whole season. It will be easy because the garlic beds will already be cover cropped until September. They also have two empty beds in the cucurbit block, which they decided to fill with extra crops: one with early beets, the other with late carrots. They will seed and weed these backup crops, which represent a little bit of extra work. However, they will only harvest them (which is a lot of work) in the event of a crop failure, or if they have a buyer (and a good price).

Field block crop maps

Once your field dates and quantities are fixed, you can draw *crop maps* for each of your blocks. A crop map is a visual representation of all the crops that will be planted in a given block during the season. It shows each bed in your block, what will be planted in it, and the planting date. Because bed and field layouts differ for every farm, no crop map template is included in this book.

Group beds by planting date to ease soil preparation and cleanup. If some beds will stay in the field longer than others, place them at the edge of a block rather than in the middle. That way, after the other crops are harvested, a larger area can be worked together. Consider what will be happening in adjacent blocks when deciding where to place late crops.

Table 4.3a and 4.3b show Bruce and Hanna's 2 mixed blocks. Each bed is filled in as the season progresses. Once they have filled the whole block, Bruce and Hanna begin the next one. They still have 5 beds to place after filling the blocks. These will be double cropped in the pea beds. The peas should be harvested and incorporated before the remaining 5 beds are planted on or after July 31.

TABLE 4.3A CROP MAP FOR BLOCK OF EARLY MIXED CROPS

BED	CROPS			
1*	01-May Peas	31-July	Carrots *	
2*	01-May Peas	31-July	Carrots *	
3*	01-May Peas	31-July	Carrots *	
4*	01-May Peas	14-Aug	Lettuce *	
5*	01-May Peas	14-Aug	Lettuce *	
6	08-May Beets			
7	08-May 50 ft Beets	50 ft Carrots		
8	08-May Carrots			
9	22-May Beans			
10	22-May Beans			
11	22-May 35 ft Lettuce	35 ft Basil	30 ft Beans	
12	05-Jun 65 ft Lettuce	35 ft Beets		
13	05-Jun Beets			
14	05-Jun Beans			
15	05-Jun 65 ft Carrots	35 ft Basil		

*Beds marked * are cropped a second time after first crop is finished.*

TABLE 4.3B CROP MAP FOR BLOCK OF LATE MIXED CROPS

BED	CROPS			
1	05-Jun Carrots			
2	05-Jun Carrots			
3	19-Jun Beans			
4	19-Jun 30 ft Basil	35 ft Lettuce	26-Jun	35 ft Lettuce
5	03-Jul Beans			
6	03-Jul Beets			
7	03-Jul Carrots			
8	03-Jul Carrots			
9	03-Jul Carrots			
10	03-Jul 35 ft Lettuce	30 ft Basil	10-Jul	35 ft Lettuce
11	17-Jul Beans			
12	17-Jul Beets			
13	17-Jul 35 ft Lettuce	35 ft Beets	30 ft Basil	
14	24-Jul 35 ft Lettuce		31-Jul	65 ft Lettuce
15	31-Jul Beets			

CROP ROTATION BASED ON FIELD BLOCKS

The blocks that you have defined are the units of your crop rotation. Now you have to place them into an actual rotation. There are several ways to do this, but the underlying principle is to avoid growing the same thing repeatedly in the same spot.

In creating your blocks, you already considered the most important elements of crop rotation: crop family, fertility requirements, and the timing of planting and harvesting. At this point you should assign an order to your blocks that will allow you to follow as many of these guidelines as possible:

- Do not return to the same crop family for 3, 4 or even 6 years. This is especially important for cucurbits, brassicas, solanacea, and alliums.
- Alternate between heavy and light feeders.
- Keep early crops together so they can be followed by a bare fallow and cover crop that will flush out late season weeds.
- Keep late season crops together so they can be preceded by a cover crop and stale seedbed to flush out early weeds.
- Over the years, alternate early and late season crops as much as possible to benefit from reduced weed pressure.
- Include as many cover crops and fallow periods as possible.
- Consider the residue levels, volunteer seeds, and uncontrolled weeds that a crop usually leaves behind.

Bruce and Hanna decide on the following rotation:

YEAR	CROP	FERTILITY
1	Solanacea and over-wintered garlic	Heavy
2	Late planted mixed crops	Light
3	Brassicas	Heavy
4	Cucurbits and Alliums	Heavy
5	Early planted mixed crops	Light
6	Cover crop and fall planted garlic	Fallow

LES JARDINS DE TESSA

FRÉDÉRIC DUHAMEL AND YOANA GARIÉPY, FRELIGHSBURG, QUEBEC

FROST FREE:
May to late
September

FARM SIZE:
14 hectares (35 acres);
7 ha in vegetables,
7 ha in cover crops

MARKETING:
CSA (320 shares),
farmers markets,
wholesale potatoes
and squash

LES JARDINS DE TESSA is renowned for its streamlined management and planning. Frédéric Duhamel grew up on an asparagus farm and studied ecology in college before starting his own farm in 1997 in Quebec's Eastern Townships.

The farm's fields are divided in 0.8 ha (1.5 acre) blocks. Frédéric and Yoana grow 2 potato blocks, 2 cucurbit blocks, 1 onion block, and 1.5 brassica blocks. They generally grow vegetables for two years followed by a cover crop for one or two years. The remaining crops are produced in smaller blocks closer to the farmhouse. He has a separate rotation for these crops.

Frédéric's rotation is not set in stone. Flexibility allows crop placement that considers soil texture and fertility, weed pressure, drainage and accessibility on a case by case basis.

Each January, over the course of three weeks, Frédéric plans the upcoming season. On a production calendar, he notes seeding dates, quantities and cultivars. From that he generates a seed order.

Since his system is now well-established, his crop planning consists of reviewing each vegetable and adapting the production calendar to solve the previous year's challenges. In his planning, Frédéric aims for a constant supply of high demand vegetables. He makes adjustments to suit consumer preferences from year to year and tries to avoid generating surpluses.

Frédéric has streamlined his production to only grow crops that work well for his equipment and land. For 10 years, he did not grow carrots because his soil and weeding equipment were not adequate for this crop. He would buy carrots from other local organic growers to put in his CSA shares. Because of the demand for fresh carrots at market, he is trialing carrots again.

Les Jardins de Tessa is highly mechanized, including a mechanical transplanter, and Farmall belly-mounted tractors used for all weeding. Changing implements on the tractors can take a lot time, so Frédéric installed a quick attach system for his main tractor tools. He groups together as many plantings as possible to reduce shuffling machines and implements. This optimizes the time that the transplanter is on the tractor and reduces travel times.

Frédéric stretches the harvest period from each planting date by using multiple varieties with different DTM. For example, in each brassica wave he plants four varieties to extend the harvest over three weeks. He also plants kohlrabi at the same time. The four broccoli varieties are seeded at the same time in the greenhouse and the kohlrabi one week later. His crop plan now includes:

- 4 beet waves (1 tp, 3 ds)
- 3 waves each of brassicas, spinach, swiss chard and carrots
- 2 fennel waves

Exceptions to his grouped plantings are beans (6 waves), and lettuces (11 waves – biweekly in spring and weekly in summer).

Frédéric trials promising new releases, especially organic varieties. He grows 3 flats of a new variety and plants it in the middle of a block (to avoid border effects). He plants 3 rows side-by-side, one with a standard variety, and 2 new ones. He compares their growth habits, uniformity, and maturation dates. Their capacity to hold in the field is very important to accommodate the time between planting different waves. He records his observations in a notebook, and uses these to choose next year's varieties.

Frédéric's biggest challenge is scheduling the spring workflow. "At the beginning of May everything needs to be seeded at once, and at the end of May everything needs to be transplanted at the same time," he says. Planning by labour availability rather than earliest crop dates helps resolve this challenge. His production calendar therefore dedicates the first week of May to planting onions and leeks; the second to early brassicas, beets, lettuce, spinach, and swiss chard; the third to potatoes; and the last week is reserved for planting frost-sensitive crops: solanaceae, melons and squash. This keeps things sane for Frédéric and his work crew.

LES JARDINS DE TESSA
FRÉDÉRIC DUHAMEL AND YOANA GARIÉPY, FRELIGHSBURG, QUEBEC

5 CHOOSE VEGETABLE VARIETIES AND FINALIZE PLANTING SCHEDULE

ONCE YOU KNOW THE TOTAL BED LENGTH for each crop, for each week of the season you'll have to divide it into smaller lengths for the different varieties you want to plant. At that point you will have your final *field planting schedule*.

CHOOSE VEGETABLE VARIETIES

COMPARING DTM
IN DIFFERENT
CATALOGUES
DTMs can be calculated from either the direct seeding date (DS) or the transplant date (TP). Check to see how the DTMs were calculated when you compare varieties. Does the seed company assume the crop will be transplanted (TP) or direct seeded (DS)? Also, check the location of the company. DTMs reflect the climatic zone where varieties are tested. Unless you live in the same zone, the DTM will likely differ from what's printed on the package.

Seeds are available from many companies and are generally sold by mail or ordered through the Internet. Request catalogues from as many seed companies as you can. The descriptions they provide are a good starting point for learning what varieties are available and how they differ from one another. Before you buy, talk to organic growers in your area and ask them where they order from and which varieties they use.

There are many reasons to choose a particular vegetable variety. Marketing concerns such as colour, flavour and storability are all very important to your clients. Yield and pest and disease resistance also affect your growing success. For crop planning purposes, there are two main considerations: climatic adaptation and days to maturity (DTM) ratings.

Climatic Adaptation
Most varieties are bred for specific weather and seasonal conditions. Make sure that for each planting, you choose varieties that are well adapted to the climatic conditions. You might not notice much difference for vegetables like carrots, but crops such as lettuce and broccoli will perform poorly if planted at the wrong time.

Days to Maturity (DTM)
Choose varieties that cover the harvest period between plantings. If you plant every 2 weeks, you will need a range of varieties with DTM that span 14 days

or so. If you plant every 4 weeks, you should target 28 days. For example, if you plant carrots every two weeks, you could choose three varieties with the following DTM: 55, 62, and 69. This would ensure constant fresh harvest for the entire 2-week harvest period. Then you'll move on to the next planting.

DTMs depend on the weather. In the heat of the summer, for example, the advertised DTM range could start sooner because vegetables – such as lettuce and broccoli – may mature faster than expected. In the fall, the DTM could be delayed, because days are shorter and temperatures colder; a radish rated for 28 days may actually take 32 or 38 days to mature.

Bruce and Hanna have chosen these lettuce varieties from several seed catalogues. DTMs (in parentheses) are from DS: Black Seeded Simpson (45), Salad Bowl (50), Red Oak (60), Jericho (57) and Winter Density (55).

Among these varieties, the difference between the longest and the shortest season is 15 days. This covers 2 weeks between lettuce planting dates. Bruce and Hanna should stagger the harvest over the 2-week harvest period.

Black Seeded Simpson, Salad Bowl, and Jericho are lettuces that perform well during the summer. Red Oak and Winter Density can tolerate colder conditions.

TRIAL NEW VARIETIES

Trialing introduces you to varieties that are new and potentially reliable. The more varieties you trial however, the less you might notice. Select crops that are known for having significant yield or production problems. That way, your trial will target the weaker links in your farm system. Highlight your reasons for trialing a specific variety so that you can evaluate it during the season.

- Grow only a small quantity of any variety you trial. If it doesn't yield much, it won't matter.
- Grow your trials next to your standard varieties for easy visual comparison.
- Try a variety in different succession plantings to see how it performs under different weather conditions.
- Avoid planting trials at the edge of fields or beds where conditions are more variable.
- Identify your trials with markers or flags so you can easily observe them through the season.

If a trial is successful, and you want to grow the variety again, plant a bit more the next year. See how it fares for a couple of years in different weather conditions. After a few seasons of growing increasing amounts, it should be clear whether a trial variety is ready to become a new standard.

FINALIZE FIELD PLANTING SCHEDULE

- Take another blank *planting schedule* template.
- Label it *Final Planting Schedule*
- Transfer the information from the *balanced block planting schedules* as follows:
  - » Enter the name of the **Crop**
  - » Transfer the bed lengths per date for that crop. If a crop is split on different block planting schedules, make sure you include them all here.
  - » On the subsequent rows, write down the varieties you wish to use. (One variety per row).
  - » Use the **Notes** column to record each variety's DTM.
  - » Divide the total bed length for each planting date between the different varieties. The bed length allotted to each variety is based on your own preferences and market knowledge.
  - » Once you have completed one crop, move on to the next.
- For each variety, add up the total bed length planted over the season. Write the result in the **Total bed length** column at the end. This column is important for the crop seed order.
- Fill out the **rows/bed** column, and the **spacing** column with the appropriate information. These will serve as reminders when you go out to plant in the field.

Once you have transferred all of your crops, you have your *final field planting schedule* in hand. You know what to plant and how much to plant every week of the season. Your crop maps created in step 4 tell you where to plant. Now you can take this schedule into Step 6, and determine how many plants to start in the greenhouse and when to start them.

STEP 5

Bruce and Hanna choose lettuce varieties for each field date:
- *May 22: They split the 35 bedft between the varieties with longest DTM since this planting is only harvested at the end of the harvest period.*
- *June 5 through July 24: They split each field date's bed lengths between the 4 summer-tolerant varieties. They do this even during the summer weekly plantings since lettuce matures very quickly.*
- *July 31: They keep three of their main varieties, and switch Jericho for Winter Density, in anticipation of colder fall weather. They shift the variety distribution towards longer DTM and cold resistant lettuces.*

TABLE 5.1: PORTION OF BRUCE AND HANNA'S FINAL FIELD PLANTING SCHEDULE

Crop	Notes	08-MAY	22-MAY	29-MAY	05-JUN	19-JUN	26-JUN	03-JUL	10-JUL	17-JUL	24-JUL	31-JUL	14-AUG	TOTAL BED LENGTH
LETTUCE			35		65	35	35	35	35	35	35	65	200	
Black Seeded Simpson	45 DTM				15	5	10	10	10	5	10	15	35	115
Salad Bowl	50 DTM				15	10	5	10	10	10	5	15		80
Red Oak	60 DTM		20		20	10	10	10	5	10	10	20	100	215
Jericho	57 DTM		15		15	10	10	5	10	10	10			85
Winter Density	55 DTM											15	65	80
BEETS		150			135		100			135	100			
Early Wonder		50			35					35				120
Detroit		50			50		50			50	50			250
Red Ace F1		50			50		50			50	50			250
TOMATOES					700									
Big Beef F1					200									200
New Girl F1					200									200
First Lady F1					200									200
Cherokee Purple					50									50
Green Zebra					50									50

ALL BED LENGTHS IN BEDFT

WALLY'S URBAN MARKET GARDEN

WALLY SATZEWICH AND GAIL VANDERSTEEN, SASKATOON, SASKATCHEWAN

FROST FREE:
mid May to early October

FARM SIZE:
3/4 acre in vegetables

MARKETING:
farmers market, restaurants

WALLY AND GAIL RUN "A MULTI-LOCATIONAL SUB-ACRE FARM." They rely on growing a quick succession of high-value crops in people's back-yards throughout the city. Wally promotes this growing method as SPIN farming (**S**mall **P**lot **IN**tensive farming).

Over a period of 20 years, their original farm grew to 20 acres. Irrigation, labour and pest control were a challenge. In 1999, they re-examined their growing model and decided to grow exclusively on small urban lots. Currently, they have 12 lots that total about 3/4 of an acre.

Farming in the city has several advantages, mainly the urban micro-climate. The gardens in Saskatoon have a mid-May to early October frost-free period – significantly longer than in the surrounding rural area. There also tends to be less pest pressure, more wind protection, and easy access to water for irrigation.

Wally and Gail specialize in quick-growing salad greens, baby greens, and micro-greens. They also distinguish themselves with spe-cialty varieties (such as golden and candy cane beets, or cipollini on-ions) and heirloom varieties of pumpkins and tomatoes.

SPIN concepts of farm management include:

- 25 ft long garden lots are divided into 3 ft beds including 2 ft grow-ing space and 1 ft path
- farm machinery consists of a rototiller and hand tools
- most beds are cropped multiple times in the season
- crops are grouped in areas depending on how often they are re-planted: full season crops, double-cropped or more frequent turn-over

Wally's crop relays revolve around baby greens and salad greens planted before and after other crops. He has been trying to shift his crop mix towards faster DTM and more dependable yields. He is currently looking to replace part of the lettuce in his salad mixes with less disease-prone crops.

Wally does not rely on a specific crop rotation but uses these guidelines:

- he avoids returning to garlic in the same spot for three years
- he monitors key crops that are susceptible to disease (such as carrots) or specific pests (especially flea beetles in arugula). When he begins to see signs of a problem, the next planting goes in a different backyard
- if he doesn't notice any problems, he doesn't worry about the crop's location. He has been growing spring spinach on the same site for 15 years, and is still satisfied

Crop planning started with notebooks but has been internalized over time. During the growing season, Wally makes mental notes of what crops sell out quickly so as to grow more the next year. However, Wally and Gail limit the amount they plant to what they know they can weed and harvest. Though they could sell more garlic, they don't grow anymore because the harvest window is so narrow. They limit their fall carrot planting to what can be harvested with hand tools.

Wally believes that new growers should start small to avoid costs and keep things under control. He says, "Maybe they should consider that small is a good place to stay."

WALLY'S URBAN MARKET GARDEN
WALLY SATZEWICH AND GAIL VANDERSTEEN, SASKATOON, SASKATCHEWAN

6 GENERATE GREENHOUSE SCHEDULES

IN CANADA, crops transplanted in the field are usually started in a greenhouse (GH). The third part of your crop plan, the greenhouse schedule, tells how many trays to seed on each of your greenhouse planting dates. As you did with the field planting schedule, fill out GH worksheets for each crop and then consolidate the information into a GH schedule.

To save space in the greenhouse, some crops are potted up (PU). Solanaceae crops, celery, celeriac, herbs, and flowers are generally potted up. They are seeded densely in a tray and then replanted into a more spacious tray.

GREENHOUSE WORKSHEET

Work backwards from the *field planting schedule* to determine greenhouse dates and number of trays to seed. The number of trays to seed depends on whether or not the crop is potted up.

GH SEEDING DATES

- Use one *GH worksheet* for each transplanted crop; label it with the crop's name.
- Transfer the data from the *field planting schedule* (step 5) as follows:
  - » For each **field date,** use a different row to list each **variety** that will be planted that week.
  - » Enter the **bed lengths, rows/bed and inrow spacing** for each variety and field date.
- Fill each of the following columns one by one:
  - » **GH Days:**
    Enter the GH Days from CHART A2. This is the number of days a crop takes from seeding until it is ready to be planted in the field.
  - » **GH Date:**
    Use a calendar and this formula:[Field Date - GH days = GH date]
- Calculate the **GH date** once for every **field date.** Apply the result to all **varieties** planted on the same day.

*Bruce and Hanna calculate GH dates on the lettuce GH worksheet. Lettuce has 28 GH days before planting out. They count that number of days backwards on a calendar to determine GH dates. Varieties with a May 22 **field date** will be seeded in the GH on April 24.*

TABLE 6.1A PARTIAL LETTUCE GREENHOUSE WORKSHEET

Example of the use of the worksheet – When you are NOT potting up

| | | | | | | | TRAYS TO SEED | | | |
VARIETY (1)	FIELD DATE (2)	GH DAYS (3)	GH DATE (4)	BED LENGTH (5)	ROWS PER BED (6)	INROW SPACING (7)	GH SF (8)	TRAY SIZE (9)	CALCULATE TRAYS (10)	ACTUAL TRAYS (11)
				bedft		ft				
Black Seeded Simpson	05-JUN	28	08-MAY	15	3	1	1.3	72	0.8	1
Salad Bowl	05-JUN	28	08-MAY	15	3	1	1.3	72	0.8	1
Red Oak	05-JUN	28	08-MAY	20	3	1	1.3	72	1.1	1
Jericho	05-JUN	28	08-MAY	15	3	1	1.3	72	0.8	1
Black Seeded Simpson	19-JUN	28	22-MAY	5	3	1	1.3	72	0.3	0.5
Salad Bowl	19-JUN	28	22-MAY	10	3	1	1.3	72	0.5	0.5
Red Oak	19-JUN	28	22-MAY	10	3	1	1.3	72	0.5	0.5
Jericho	19-JUN	28	22-MAY	10	3	1	1.3	72	0.5	0.5

TRAYS TO SEED IF YOU ARE NOT POTTING UP

If you are NOT potting up, fill out columns 8 to 11 only.

Greenhouse Safety Factors (GH SF):
A factor of 1.3 should offset the losses caused by uneven watering and temperature variations.

Tray Size:
Enter the value from CHART A2. This is the number of cells in the GH trays. You can also use open trays: these are trays with no cells. In this case, estimate the number of seeds you'll seed to get a size.

*At la Ferme Coopéra-tive Tourne-Sol, onions are seeded into large open styrofoam trays. Seven rows of 72 seeds are seeded in each flat. The **tray size** we use is 500 (7 * 72 = about 500).*

Calculated trays:

[(Bed length * rows/bed ÷ inrow spacing) * GH SF ÷ tray size = calculated trays]

Actual trays:

Round off the number of trays

If you are seeding into trays that will go into the field without potting up, this is the final step on the GH worksheet.

How many trays of Jericho lettuce will Bruce and Hanna need for their May 22nd Field Date?

- *Bed Length: 15 ft*
- *Rows/Bed: 3*
- *Inrow spacing: 1 ft*
- ***GH SF** of 1.3*
- ***Tray Size**: 72*
- ***Calculate trays**: [(15 ft * 3 rows/bed ÷ 1 ft) * 1.3 ÷ 72 = 0.8 trays to seed]*
- ***Actual Trays**: They round this off to 1 tray.*

Celery and celeriac trays to pot up

Ferme Coopérative Tourne-Sol

STEP 6

TABLE 6.1B TOMATO GREENHOUSE WORKSHEET

Example of the use of the worksheet – When you ARE potting up

							TRAYS TO PU				TRAYS TO SEED			
1	2	3	4	5	6	7	8	9	10	11	12	13	14	15
VARIETY	FIELD DATE	GH DAYS	GH DATE	BED LENGTH	ROWS PER BED	INROW SPACING	GH SF	TRAY SIZE	CALCULATE TRAYS	ACTUAL TRAYS	GH SF	SEEDED TRAY SIZE	CALCULATE TRAYS	ACTUAL TRAYS
				bedft		ft								
Big Beef	29 MAY	42	17 APR	200	1	1.5	1.1	50	2.9	3	1.3	98	1.99	2
New Girl	29 MAY	42	17 APR	200	1	1.5	1.1	50	2.9	3	1.3	98	1.99	2
First Lady	29 MAY	42	17 APR	200	1	1.5	1.1	50	2.9	3	1.3	98	1.99	2
Cherokee Purple	29 MAY	42	17 APR	50	1	1.5	1.1	50	0.7	1	1.3	98	0.66	0.7
Green Zebra	29 MAY	42	17 APR	50	1	1.5	1.1	50	0.7	0.5	1.3	98	0.33	0.3

TRAYS TO SEED IF YOU ARE POTTING UP

First, calculate how many trays to pot up (columns 8 to 11). Then, calculate how many trays to seed (columns 12 to 15) so that you have enough plants to pot up.

GH SF: Young plants are quite resilient, so there should be little loss at the pot up stage. Enter a value of 1.1.
Tray size: Enter the value from CHART A2.
Calculated trays:
[(Bed length * rows/bed ÷ inrow spacing) * GH SF ÷ tray size = trays to pot up]
Actual trays: Round off the number of **calculated trays**.

TRAYS TO SEED

GH SF: Use a minimum of 1.3. For the tiniest herb seeds and celery seeds, you might want to use a safety factor of 2.

Tray Size: Enter the tray size you will initially seed into. Choose open trays or trays with smaller cells than those you will be potting into.

Calculate trays:
[(Trays to PU * PU tray size) * GH SF ÷ seeded tray size = trays to seed]
Actual trays: Round off the number of **calculated trays**.

How many trays do Bruce and Hanna need to pot up and seed of Big Beef tomatoes? Notice they use different tray sizes for both operations.

Trays to pot up:

- *Bed Length: 200 ft*
- *Rows/Bed: 1*
- *Inrow Spacing: 1.5 ft*
- *GH SF: 1.1*
- *PU Tray Size: 50*
- *Calculate trays: [(200 ft * 1 row/bed ÷ 1.5 ft) * 1.1 ÷ 50 = 2.93 trays to pot up]*
- *Actual trays : They round this to 3 actual trays to pot up*

Trays to seed:

- *GH SF: 1.3*
- *Seeded Tray Size: 98*
- *Calculate Trays: [(3 trays to PU * 50 cells/tray) * 1.3 ÷ 98 cells/tray =1.99 trays]*
- *Actual trays: They round this to 2 actual trays to seed.*

MAKE GREENHOUSE SCHEDULE

Once you have a greenhouse worksheet for each GH crop, you can prepare your greenhouse schedule. The process is similar to the one you used to prepare your field schedules:

- Enter **crop, variety** and **tray size** columns with the crops and varieties from your ***GH worksheets.***
- Fill out the **seeds/cell** column using CHART A2. For some vegetable species seeding multiple seeds in a cell will help offset erratic germination due to temperature or seed quality. Any additional seedlings per cell can be thinned.
- Indicate the **GH dates** when you plan to seed in the greenhouse.
- For each date, write down how many trays of each variety you will be seeding.
- For each variety, add the **total seeded trays.**

Use the last two columns for potting up information.

- Enter the number of trays to pot up in the **PU trays** column, and the **PU tray size**.

This chart does not show *when* to pot up. That's something you should do when you think the plant is ready.

You now have your greenhouse schedule. It summarizes how much of each variety to plant every week in the GH. The **total seeded trays** and **seeds/cell** columns will be the starting point for your *seed order*.

TABLE 6.3 BRUCE AND HANNA'S PARTIAL GH PLANTING SCHEDULE

CROP	VARIETY	TRAY SIZE	SEEDS PER CELL	24-APR	08-MAY	22-MAY	29-MAY	05-JUN	12-JUN	19-JUN	26-JUN	03-JUL	17-JUL	TOTAL SEEDED TRAYS	PU TRAYS	PU TRAY SIZE
				GH PLANTING DATE												
Lettuce	Black Seeded Simpson	72	3		1	0.5	0.5	0.5	0.5	0.5	0.5	1	2	7		
Lettuce	Salad Bowl	72	3		1	0.5	0.5	0.5	0.5	0.5	0.5	1		5		
Lettuce	Red Oak	72	3	1	1	0.5	0.5	0.5	0.5	0.5	0.5	1	5.5	11.5		
Lettuce	Jericho	72	3	1	1	0.5	0.5	0.5	0.5	0.5	0.5			5		
Lettuce	Winter Density	72	3									1	3.5	4.5		
TOTAL TRAYS				2	4	2	2	2	2	2	2	4	11	33		
Tomato	Big Beef F1	98	1	2										2	3	50
Tomato	New Girl F1	98	1	2										2	3	50
Tomato	First Lady F1	98	1	2										2	3	50
Tomato	Cherokee Purple	98	1	0.7										0.7	1	50
Tomato	Green Zebra	98	1	0.3										0.3	0.5	50
TOTAL TRAYS				7	0	0	0	0	0	0	0	0	0	7	10.5	

ANN SLATER'S FRESH ORGANIC VEGETABLES

ANN SLATER, ST-MARY'S, ONTARIO

FROST FREE:
late May to late
September

FARM SIZE:
1.5 acres in vegetables

MARKETING:
CSA (35 shares),
farmers market,
restaurants

ANN SLATER has been growing vegetables for 25 years, in 1.5 acres of gardens on her brother's organic dairy farm. She keeps a flock of sheep on the farm to produce manure for the garden.

Double-cropping has allowed her to keep the land area small. Ann transplants most crops rather than direct seeding them. Since transplanted crops are quicker to harvest, the area they occupy can be re-planted sooner. Ann transplants lettuces, mustards, and escaroles for salad greens. She also transplants turnips seeded 5–6 seeds/cell without thinning.

Ann tracks sales throughout the year and makes mental notes of changes in demand. At the end of the season, her sales totals and extensive production notes help her determine any adjustments for next season.

Her garden area is in four sections, each with a map showing three to four blocks that are rotated by considering crop family, growing habits and time to plant or harvest. Ann says, "Crop planning is a balancing act of market demands, crop rotations and the land's needs."

She emphasizes the importance of keeping good notes "because you won't remember it all." Her notes guide her in deciding next year's planting schedule, especially how late she can squeeze in another crop for late fall harvests. Since new farmers don't have their own knowledge and history recorded yet, she advises, "Don't be afraid to call people who have done it and pick our brains. I might not be able to tell you how many bedfeet of beans I grew, but I know how much bean seed I planted for my market objectives, and you can use that to figure out your own space and seed needs."

7 FILL OUT A SEED ORDER

N OW YOU NEED TO ORDER ENOUGH SEED to carry out your greenhouse and field plans. Your seed worksheet will help you calculate how many seeds you need based on your field planting and GH schedules. Use it to compare seed formats and prices in different seed catalogues. As you choose seed quantities from various catalogues, you can fill out your seed order.

SEED WORKSHEET

- Enter the name of each **crop** and each **variety** listed on your *field planting schedule.*
- Indicate whether the crop is direct-seeded (**DS**) or transplanted (**TP**).

The next column header on the worksheet is split into two rows; follow the top for DS crops and the bottom for TP crops.

SEED COUNT FOR DIRECT-SEEDED (DS) CROPS

For each variety:
- Enter the **bed length** and **rows/bed** from your *field planting schedule* (step 5).
- Enter the **seeding rate** for each crop from CHART A1. This information is also available in most seed catalogues. You can get a more precise seeding rate by calibrating your own seeder (see sidebar). Use seeds/m for bedm and seeds/ft for bedft.
- Enter your seed safety factor. A **seed SF** of 1.3 should keep you from running out of seed. In most cases you can use this seed again the next year.
- Calculate the **Seed Count**
  [Bed Length * Rows/Bed * Seeding Rate * Seed SF = Seed Count]

How many Early Wonder Tall Top beet seeds do Bruce and Hanna need?
Bed length: 120 bedft over the season
- *Rows/bed: 3 rows*
- *Seeding rate of 16 seeds/ft*
- *Seed SF of 1.3.*
- *Seed count: [120 bedft * 3 rows/bed * 16 seeds/ft * 1.3 = 7,488 seeds needed]*

CALIBRATE YOUR SEEDERS

Calibrate each of your seeders using this formula:

[Number of seeds ÷ Distance seeder travelled = Seeding rate]

Repeat this calculation for each setting on your seeder.

To figure out the **number of seeds**
- Fill the hopper on the seeder
- Raise the seeder over a container
- Turn the drive wheel a fixed number of turns.
- Count the seeds that dropped into the container

To figure out the **distance traveled**:
- Measure the circumference of the seeder's drive wheel.
- Multiply the circumference by the number of turns you rotated the wheel

Ferme Coopérative Tourne-Sol

Filling a seed hopper

Bruce and Hanna use a pinpoint seeder to seed arugula. There are three holes on the pinpoint seeder. They decide to use the medium hole

HOLE SIZE	NUMBER OF SEEDS	DISTANCE TRAVELED	SEEDING RATE
Small	21	1.44 ft (0.44 m)	15 seeds/ft (48 seeds/m)
Medium	42	1.44 ft (0.44 m)	29 seeds/ft (95 seeds/m)
Big	136	1.44 ft (0.44 m)	94 seeds/ft (309 seeds/m)

Fred Duhamel of Les Jardins de Tessa fills his seed hopper with a measuring cup. He empties his hopper into a measuring cup when he's finished seeding. Using a scale and the seeds/gram for that crop he can figure out his seeding rates.

SEED COUNT FOR TRANSPLANTED (TP) CROPS

For each transplanted variety:

- Enter the **trays seeded**, **tray size** and **seeds/cell** from your *GH schedule* in step 6.
- Enter your seed safety factor (**seed SF**). A seed SF of 1.3 should be adequate.
- Calculate the **Seed Count**:

[Trays Seeded * Tray Size * Seeds/Cell * Seed SF = Seed Count]

How many Jericho Lettuce seeds will Bruce and Hanna need?
- *Trays seeded: 5 trays over whole season*
- *Tray size: 72 cells/tray*
- *Seeds/Cell: 3 seeds/cell*
- *Seed SF of 1.3*
- *Seed Count: 5 trays * 72 cells/tray * 3 sds/cell * 1.3 = 1,404 seeds needed*

CONVERT SEED COUNTS INTO WEIGHTS

Seeds are sold by seed count or by weight (ounces, grams or pounds). It is easier to compare different seed packet formats and prices if you know the equivalent weights for your seed counts.

- Enter the **Seeds/gram** from CHART A1 or A2. This value corresponds to an average seed density for a crop. Seed catalogues sometimes list precise seed densities for a variety. If they do, use the value provided by the seed company instead of the average.
- Convert **seed count** to **Grams** : Seed count ÷ seeds/g = Grams
- To convert **Grams** to **Ounces:** Grams ÷ 28 = Ounces
- To convert **Ounces** to **Pounds:** Ounces ÷ 16 = Pounds

Hanna and Bruce convert their Jericho seed count
- *Seed count: 1,404 seeds.*
- *Grams: 1,404 lettuce seeds ÷ 800 seeds/g =1.76 g*
- *Ounces: 1.76 g ÷ 28 =0.06 ounces*
- *Pounds: 0.06 oz ÷ 16 = 0.004 pounds*

Conversions for other seed densities

(seeds/oz) ÷ 28 = (seeds/g)

(seeds/lb) ÷ 454 = (seeds/g)

TABLE 7.1 PARTIAL SEED WORKSHEET

CROP VARIETY	FOR DS / FOR TP	BED LENGTH / TRAYS SEEDED	ROWS PER BED / TRAY SIZE	SEED RATE / SEEDS PER CELL	SEED SF	SEED COUNT	SEEDS PER GRAM	GRAMS	OUNCES	POUNDS
BEETS										
Early Wonder	DS	120	3	16	1.3	7,488	55	136.15	4.86	0.30
Detroit	DS	250	3	16	1.3	15,600	55	265.91	9.50	0.59
Red Ace F1	DS	250	3	16	1.3	15,600	55	265.91	9.50	0.59
TOMATOES										
Big Beef F1	TP	2	98	1	1.3	255	350	0.73	0.03	
New Girl F1	TP	2	98	1	1.3	255	350	0.73	0.03	
First Lady F1	TP	2	98	1	1.3	255	350	0.73	0.03	
Cherokee Purple	TP	0.7	98	1	1.3	89	350	0.25	0.01	
Green Zebra	TP	0.3	98	1	1.3	38	350	0.11	0.005	
LETTUCE										
Black Seeded Simpson	TP	7	72	3	1.3	1,966	800	2.46	0.09	0.01
Salad Bowl	TP	5	72	3	1.3	1,404	800	1.76	0.06	
Red Oak	TP	11.5	72	3	1.3	3,229	800	4.04	0.14	0.01
Jericho	TP	5	72	3	1.3	1,404	800	1.76	0.06	
Winter Density	TP	4.5	72	3	1.3	1,264	800	1.58	0.06	

WHEN EVERY SEED COUNTS

Plan carefully with expensive seed. Greenhouse tomatoes, greenhouse cucumbers, and some hybrid seed can be costly. Do not use more than 1 seed/cell, use a seed SF of 1.1, and don't spill the packet on the ground by accident. Start additional trays of less expensive seed as a backup for these varieties.

THE ORGANIC COLUMN

When the seed you buy is certified organic, put a check-mark in the **organic** *column of your seed order. This will make your seed order very useful when you file your organic certification papers.*

Verify your Certifier's policy about organic seed.

BUYING TRANSPLANTS

Growers sometimes order transplants instead of starting them themselves. Some nurseries will start your seeds for you; you can give them your greenhouse schedule as a guide. Others only have certain varieties available at certain times. Make sure the varieties you choose and your field planting dates fit the nursery's schedule. Either way, your tray size (step 6) should correspond to the nursery's specifications.

CHOOSE SEED FORMAT AND SEED QUANTITIES

Spread your seed catalogues out on the table and look at how each variety you want is sold. Use the seed count and weights from the seed worksheet to decide which seed packet format meets your needs. Consider **price**, **quantity**, and **source** when choosing what to buy.

Price
Shopping with price in mind can save you money. Different catalogues often sell the same varieties for different prices.

Quantity
You can usually get a discount when you buy larger quantities. If you can afford it, you'll save money by purchasing a bigger packet of seeds than you need, and storing them for future years. Just remember that not all seeds store well. Use leek, onion, and parsnip seeds the year they're bought; germination drops significantly if you wait.

Source
Be careful when buying seeds from a catalogue or company you don't know. If it's your first time ordering from a particular company, ask other growers what they think about the seed quality. Start with a smaller order. If you are satisfied, add to your order next year.

FILL OUT SEED ORDER

Take a blank *seed order* template. On each row:
- Enter the **crop** and **variety**
- List the **seed catalogue** and **item number**.
- If the seed is certified organic, check that off in the **organic** column.
- Enter the **quantity** and **format** of each packet you have selected.
- Enter the cost in Canadian or U.S. dollars depending on where the seed company is located.
- Calculate the **Total** using this formula:
  [Quantity * Unit Canadian $ = Total $]
  Or
  [Quantity * Unit US $ * exchange rate = Total $]

After you complete your seed order transfer the information onto separate sheets corresponding to each seed company. This will make it easy to place your seed order by phone, Internet, or mail.

Order your seeds on time. Seeds *do* sell out and you might have to settle for varieties you don't know or that don't perform well.

TABLE 7.2 BRUCE AND HANNA'S PARTIAL SEED ORDER

CROP VARIETY	SEED CATALOGUE	ITEM NUMBER	ORGANIC	QTY	FORMAT	$CAN	$US	TOTAL $CAN
BEETS								
Early Wonder				1	1/4 lb			0
Detroit				1	1 lb			0
Red Ace F1				15	1,000 sds			0
TOMATOES								
Big Beef F1				1	1/16 oz			0
New Girl F1				1	1/16 oz			0
First Lady F1				1	1/16 oz			0
Cherokee Purple				1	0.5g			0
Green Zebra				1	0.1g			0
LETTUCE								
Black Seeded Simpson				1	1/8 oz			0
Salad Bowl				1	1/8 oz			0
Red Oak				1	1/8 oz			0
Jericho				1	1/8 oz			0
Winter Density				1	1/8 oz			0

WIENS SHARED FARM
DAN AND WILMA WIENS, ST-GERMAIN, MANITOBA

FROST FREE:
mid-May to mid-September

FARM SIZE:
40 acres; 10-12 acres in vegetables

MARKETING:
farmers market, 40 share CSA

DAN AND WILMA WIENS grew their first crops in 1980, but it wasn't until 1990 that they were farming steadily. Their overseas involvement in agricultural development, and Dan's work with the Mennonite Central committee during the winter, are both part of their deep commitment to global food justice.

Pioneers in the Canadian CSA movement since 1992, Dan and Wilma had 200 CSA shares at one time. Currently, they run a 40-share CSA and also sell their produce at a farmers market.

Labour is a central concern in planning for the coming year. This year, Dan and Wilma will construct a building with a wash station, vegetable storage, and living quarters for apprentices. A building project of this magnitude will impact the time they have to take care of the fields. During the winter, Dan and Wilma hope to meet with next year's apprentices to gauge their commitment and help shape their crop plan.

Dan and Wilma do most of their crop planning in their head, based on their many years of experience. Dan says he appreciates on-line seed companies that keep track of his previous year's seed order. By signing into his account, he can start with last year's order and tweak the amounts. He increases the seed quantities for items that ran short, and reduces those that he had in abundance.

8 MAKE A FIELD OPERATIONS CALENDAR

THE LAST PIECE OF YOUR CROP PLAN is your field operations calendar. Your planting schedules and crop maps focus on when, where and how much you will be planting. You'll use your field operation calendar to lay out the steps you need to ensure your beds are ready when it is time to plant.

GENERAL FIELD OPERATIONS

Your plan has to account for two field operations: ground preparation and fertility management.

GROUND PREPARATION

To prepare a good seedbed you will start with a primary tillage pass, then a few secondary tillage passes; this will produce a nice planting bed. Once your bed is ready you can stale seed it to flush out weeds.

Primary Tillage

Primary Tillage (also called deep tillage) works the soil 6 to 12" (15 to 30 cm) deep to incorporate residues, break up sub soil compaction, provide soil aeration, improve drainage, and increase the depth of soil fertility.[1]
Tools for primary tillage include:
   Tractor tools: mouldboard plow, chisel plow, and offset disk harrow
   Walking tractors: these are difficult to till with at this depth; use a broadfork

Secondary Tillage

Secondary Tillage works the top few inches of soil with successive machine passes. This breaks up soil clumps, incorporates surface residues and sets up a good planting bed. Small seeded DS crops like carrots or salad greens benefit from a very finely prepared seedbed.
   Tractor tools: Disk harrow, C-tine and S-tine cultivator, rototiller
   Walking tractors: rototiller, hand rakes

1   Coleman, Eliot. 1995. *The New Organic Grower.* Chelsea Green Publishing

Stale Seed Bedding

Stale Seed Bedding is the term for letting a prepared seedbed lie fallow prior to planting. During this time, you let weed seeds germinate so there is an opportunity to eliminate them with light equipment. This reduces subsequent weed pressure in the crop. Stale seed bedding can be done in two ways:

- By gently working the soil with a tine weeder or other light tractor implement. It could also be worked at a very shallow depth with a manual rototiller. Only disturb the top 1 inch (2 cm) of soil to avoid bringing new weed seeds to the soil surface.
- By burning the emerging weeds with a flame weeder.

FERTILITY MANAGEMENT

Vegetables need a healthy soil system to thrive. Compost or manure will help meet their basic fertility needs and will add organic matter to the soil. Cover crops can also provide fertility in addition to many other benefits. Plan your practices ahead of time, and include them in your field operations calendar.

Spreading compost

Compost can be added at any point during secondary tillage. If the compost has a lot of bedding or other high carbon material, let it decompose in the soil for 4 to 6 weeks prior to planting. If your compost is fresh and high in nitrogen, you can plant as soon as your seedbed is ready.

Compost can also be spread prior to seeding a cover crop. The cover crop will catch the nutrients as it grows and will later release them when it is incorporated.

Spreading Manure

Manure can be used as a fertility source but it must be applied long before vegetable crops will be planted (verify with your organic certifier). Cover crops seeded immediately after spreading manure will keep most of the nutrients from being lost to leaching.

Cover Crops

Cover crops can be grown before or after a vegetable crop. Cover crops improve soil tilth, add fertility, help reduce the weed seed bank, and diversify the farm ecosystem. Cover crops with a lot of biomass should be incorporated 5 weeks prior to planting to make sure they have sufficient time to decompose.

Three cover crop combinations work well in Canadian climates:

- **Oats and peas** can be seeded in the spring as soon as the soil can be worked, and tilled under near the beginning of July. They can also be seeded in August or early September. Oats and peas winterkill in most of Canada. Seed 35–75 lbs/acre (40–85 kg/ha) of oats with 40 lbs/acre (45 kg/ha) of peas.

- **Buckwheat** can be seeded from end of May until early September. It should be incorporated no later than 6 weeks after it is seeded to avoid it going to seed. Buckwheat is easily killed by frost. Seed buckwheat at 48–70 lbs/acre (53–80 kg/ha) with a seed drill, or broadcast 50–90 lbs/acre (55–100 kg/ha).

- **Rye and clover** can be planted from August to the beginning of October. Rye overwinters easily, providing ground cover the following spring. Select a type of clover that will overwinter in your area. The clover will fix nitrogen and enrich the soil for the following year. Rye can be difficult to incorporate, especially with walking tractors. Be sure your equipment can do the job before using rye widely on your farm. Seed rye at 60 lbs/acre (78 kg/ha) with 4–8 lbs/acre (4.5–9 kg/ha) of a clover. [2]

TOURNE-SOL COOPERATIVE FARM GROUND PREPARATION SCHEDULE

Compost or manure is spread once every three years over a green manure block. Spreading is done in late summer before planting a fall cover crop. Crops will only be planted the following spring or summer. Spreading in the summer leaves the Tourne-Sol farmers time to focus on seedbed preparation when the spring weather is favourable.
Seedbed preparation begins 5 weeks prior to planting.

- **Five weeks prior:** *Cover crops are incorporated. This is done with a mouldboard plow, a chisel, or a heavy set of disks, depending on the amount of surface residue.*
- **Four weeks prior**: *The soil is disked.*
- **Three weeks prior**: *The ground is worked with disk harrows or an S-tine cultivator depending on how rough the surface is.*
- **Two weeks prior:** *Prepare final seedbed with rototiller (or occasionally an S-tine cultivator for TP crops).*
- **One week prior:** *Stale seed bed with tine weeder.*
- **Planting week:** *Stale seed bed just before seeding or transplanting.*

Starting seedbed preparation five weeks prior to actually planting provides flexibility to deal with unexpected weather events. If it rains a lot and you have to skip a week or two of ground work, there is still time to catch up.

---

2 Sarrantonio, Marianne. 1994. *Northeast Cover Crop Handbook*. Rodale Institute. Sustainable Agriculture Network. 2007. *Managing Cover Crop Profitably*, Handbook Series Book 9. www.sare.org/publications/index.htm]

FIELD OPERATION CALENDAR

TABLE.1 FIELD OPERATION CALENDAR *A field operation calendar for Bruce and Hanna's two mixed blocks using La Ferme Coopérative Tournesol's field operations schedule.*

BLOCK	BED NUMBER	FIELD OPERATION DATE																								
		01-MAY	08-MAY	15-MAY	22-MAY	29-MAY	05-JUN	12-JUN	19-JUN	26-JUN	03-JUL	10-JUL	17-JUL	24-JUL	31-JUL	07-AUG	14-AUG	21-AUG	28-AUG	04-SEP	11-SEP	18-SEP	25-SEP	02-OCT	09-OCT	16-OCT
5 EARLY MIXED	1 TO 3	PL												D/R	PL											
5 EARLY MIXED	4 TO 5	PL												D/R			PL									
5 EARLY MIXED	6 TO 8	C/R	PL																RC							
5 EARLY MIXED	9 TO 11	C	D/R	SS	PL														RC							
5 EARLY MIXED	12 TO 15	C	D	D	R	SS	PL												RC							
2 LATE MIXED	1 TO 2	C	D	D	R	SS	PL												OP							
2 LATE MIXED	3 TO 4			C	D	D	R	SS	PL												OP					
2 LATE MIXED	5 TO 11	OP				C	D	D	R	SS	PL												OP			
2 LATE MIXED	12 TO 14	OP						C	D	D	R	SS	PL													
2 LATE MIXED	15	OP							C	D	D	R	SS	PL												

C: chisel or plow; D: disk or S-tine cultivator; R: rototiller or S-tine cultivator; SS: stale seed bed Pl: plant vegetable; OP: plant oats and peas; B: plant buckwheat; RC: plant rye and clover
Shaded squares indicate a crop or cover crop has been planted.

All the steps involved in your bed preparation can be shown in a field operations calendar.

- Begin with a blank *field operations calendar* template
- Write in the dates of each week of the growing season
- Transfer the data from each block's *crop map*.
  - » Use a row for each **field date**.
  - » Enter the **block** name or number and which **beds** are planted on that **field date**.
  - » Indicate when you will be planting in the appropriate **field operation date** column.
- Highlight all the weeks from planting until the expected last harvest for those beds. This will help you visualise when the ground is cropped.
- Indicate your seedbed preparation steps in the calendar. Working backwards from your planting week, write in what operation you would like to do each week. Adapt this sequence for seasonal constraints.
- Assign a cover crop to grow before and after the period dedicated to field preparation and crop growing. When assigning cover crops in the fall, consider the crop planned for the following year:
  - » If it will be planted early, choose a cover crop that will winterkill.
  - » If it will be planted in mid June or later, you can use an overwintering cover crop.

This is the last piece of your crop plan. At this point, you have navigated through your whole growing season on paper or computer. The next step will be to make sure that out in the field, everything goes according to plan.

ORDER COVER CROP SEED

Area to be seeded to cover crop in the *field operations calendar*:

[(Qty beds * bed width (m) * bed length (m)) ÷ 10,000 m^2 = Area (ha)]

[(Qty beds * bed width (ft) * bed length (ft)) ÷ 43,560 sq ft = Area (acres)]

Quantity of seed to order:
[Area * Seeding rate * Seed SF = Seed Weight]

Choose your seed SF according to how precise your seeding tools are, and how expensive the seed is.

Bruce and Hanna have 22 beds of oats and peas in their mixed blocks.

Area in oats and peas:
[22 beds * 5 ft * 100 ft ÷ 43,560 sqft = 0.2 acres of oats and peas]

Quantity of seed to purchase:
[0.2 acres * 75 lbs/acre * 1.3 = 19.5 lbs of oats]
[0.2 acres * 45 lbs/acre * 1.3 = 11.7 lbs of peas]

BRIGHT FARM
BREE EAGLE, SALT SPRING ISLAND, British Columbia

FROST FREE:
early March to mid
October

FARM SIZE:
10 acres; 2 acres in
vegetables, 2 acres
in apples, .75 acre
in garlic

MARKETING:
two farmers
markets,
restaurants and
grocery stores

BREE EAGLE runs a family farm with her parents who started Bright Farm in 1992.

Bree uses maps to keep exact records of what happened in the fields. During the winter, she uses the maps to set next year's crop plan. She also uses spreadsheets on the computer to compile all crop sales and analyze the gross sales from each crop. This data helps Bree and her parents determine where in the market there is room for expansion; they change their crop mix accordingly.

Bree also uses a 10-year day planner. Each page corresponds to the same date over 10 years. This makes it easy to compare previous years with the current year when planning.

Bree makes a point of noting her observations on what to repeat and what to avoid in future. Using this long-range format of day planner has made setting seasonal and weekly tasks much simpler.

9 CARRY OUT THE CROP PLAN

After you've built a crop plan that meets your financial objectives, you'll need to keep it on hand to guide you through your season. To benefit from your plan and improve it, record what actually happens. You should also make sure it stays on track. When things don't go as planned, you'll have to adapt your crop plan as needed.

How to use your crop plan

At the start of every workweek consult your crop plan to see what has to be done. Make a "to do list" for the week based on your field planting schedule, your field operations calendar, and your greenhouse schedule.

Print out all your schedules, and keep them in a binder so you can refer to them easily. Write your "to do list" on a large backboard in the barn for the whole team to see. Finally, post a field map beside the blackboard so your work crew knows the location of all the crops in the field.

Ferme Coopérative Tourne-Sol

To do lists on blackboards.

STEP 9

RECORD WHAT ACTUALLY HAPPENS

A lot needs to get done in the heat of the summer sun. Unfortunately, record-keeping often sinks to the bottom of the to-do list and sometimes even drops right off. Don't let that happen. When it's time to review your season and improve your farm and crop plan, you will appreciate the effort you made to maintain careful records.

How do you develop good record keeping habits? Start before the growing season. During the winter, as you dream about the coming growing season:
- Decide what records to keep
- Design your record sheets and print enough copies for the whole summer
- Organize your sheets into binders or notebooks and find a place to keep them where they will be convenient to fill out, and protected from weather and rodents.

Make sure everyone on your crew knows how to fill out your record sheets and the degree of detail you want. The more people who are involved in record keeping, the clearer and more organized your records and directions should be.

Be sure to keep precise greenhouse records, field planting records, field maps, harvest records and sales records. They will help you keep track of your crop plan so you can easily monitor and improve it.

Greenhouse records

Greenhouse records show how many trays of each variety you seeded and on what date. They also show tray size, the number of seeds per cell and any potting-up information. You can either record all the crops and varieties on the same sheets in chronological order, or you can record each crop or block on separate sheets. (See Template 9.1)

Full size templates can be downloaded from the COG website www.cog.ca

TEMPLATE 9.1 – GREENHOUSE RECORD SHEET									YEAR:_____.
			SEEDING			POTTING UP			
GH SEED DATE	CROP	VARIETY	TRAY SIZE	NO. OF TRAYS	SEEDS PER CELL	POT UP DATE	TRAY SIZE	NO. OF TRAYS	NOTES

CROP PLANNING

Field planting records

Field planting records show the bed lengths that you planted of each variety and the dates you planted them along with whether the crop is DS or TP, the number of rows per bed, the spacing, and how the seeder was adjusted. Again, you can choose to organize these records alphabetically, in chronological order, by family or by block. (See Template 9.2)

TEMPLATE 9.2 — FIELD PLANTING RECORD SHEET   BLOCK:_____ YEAR:_____.

FIELD PLANT DATE	DS TP	CROP	VARIETY	LOCATION	SPACING/ SEEDER	ROWS	BED LENGTH	NOTES

Field maps

Field maps show which portion of each bed was seeded with which variety, and on which planting date. Draw a graph of your standard field block with the number of beds it includes on a piece of paper. Photocopy and fill in with information about the rows and beds that were planted (varieties, bedlength, location, dates). Use one page per field block.

Harvest records

Harvest records show how much of each crop/variety was harvested on each harvest day. They should also show which planting was harvested. To keep track of plantings you can name them (Brassica 1, Lettuce 5, Roots 3) or use a block and bed number (block 5 bed 4). To compare yields of specific varieties record their harvest data separately.

Record harvest data for all crops on the same sheet each week (template 9.3) or use separate sheets to record the harvest data for one crop for the whole season (template 9.4).

Using separate sheets (9.4) is easier for analyzing data; using one sheet (9.3) makes it easier to see whether everything has been recorded that week.

TEMPLATE 9.3 — HARVEST RECORD SHEET — BY WEEK   YEAR:_____.

CROP	VARIETY	UNIT	BED NO.	MON & TUES	BED NO.	WED & THURS	BED NO.	FRIDAY

TEMPLATE 9.4 — HARVEST RECORD SHEET — BY CROP   YEAR:_____.

				DATES									
CROP	VARIETY	UNIT	BED NO.										

Sales records

Sales records are tailored to your distribution methods.

- *Market sheets* record how much of each crop you brought to market, how much you brought back, and the unit price. (See Template 9.5)
- *CSA sheets* record the content and cost of the vegetables in your CSA basket for each week of the season. If you have several basket sizes (large and small share) you may want to have one sheet for each. (See Template 9.6)

TEMPLATE 9.5 — MARKET RECORD SHEET   DATE:_____.

MARKET: _____.   TOTAL $ SOLD: _____.

CROP	UNIT	PRICE	PLANNED HARVEST	ACTUAL HARVEST	END	SOLD	NOTES

TEMPLATE 9.6 — CSA RECORD SHEET   DATE:_____.

CSA DROP-OFF: _____.

PLANNED HARVEST	ACTUAL HARVEST	ITEM NO.	CROP	UNIT	PRICE	NOTES

MONITOR YOUR CROP PLAN AS IT UNFOLDS

Your crop plan reflects what you would like to see happen, but how will that differ from what actually occurs? Once the season starts you will need to observe and then compare what you see to what you had projected.

Observe what is going on

BE ON THE LOOKOUT FOR...
- *weed pressure*
- *soil dryness and whether irrigation is needed*
- *emergence of direct seeded crops*
- *whether seedbeds are ready to plant*
- *disease and insect pressure*
- *general health and growth of crops*
- *crop maturity*

A great farmer needs great observation skills. What you see when you're working in the field reveals how your crop plan is unfolding and guides you as you carry out your plans. You won't see everything if the only time you have to observe is when you're multi-tasking. Instead, make time in your weekly schedule for a field walk, where the only thing you do is watch. You can do this in the morning before the crew arrives or at the end of the day. A field walk can also be a good group activity. Different eyes notice different things. It also helps your farm team see the bigger picture on the farm.

Whether you're on a field walk, or simply observing while you carry on other jobs, keep a notepad in your pocket. If anything catches your eye, make a note of it and follow-up later.

Compare your Season with your Projections

In addition to field observations, you should regularly compare your records with your crop plan. Do your current harvests match your harvest plan? Are you meeting your weekly financial targets?

If the answer is no, try to figure out why. Are fertility problems, pests or the weather contributing to your shortfall? Could any of your crop planning assumptions, such as yield or safety factors be incorrect? Try to uncover the cause of serious discrepancies so that you can avoid them when planning for next season. Keeping notes will help you to remember.

ADAPT YOUR CROP PLAN IF NEEDED

When major crop plan or field layout changes are needed on the farm, Frédéric Duhamel takes his time to work them out. First, he sends his crew to do something else for the day. Then, later that night, he sits down, and looks over his long-term rotation and crop plan, and makes a decision carefully. The next morning, he is ready with clear instructions for his workers.

When your season results deviate from your crop plan, you need to intervene, but how? There is no single response to the many things that can go awry on your farm. Here are some common situations and suggestions as to how a farmer could respond.

Poor seed germination

If a direct seeded crop germinates badly and you end up with a poor stand, do you keep the crop or not? To decide, balance the importance of having a *good* harvest with having an *on-time* harvest. If you keep the planting, yields will be low, but you will still have to weed the crop as if it had germinated nicely. If you till it in and reseed it, your harvest will be delayed.

Bad seedbed

Planting into a seedbed that's full of clumps, residues, or weeds could be worse than not planting at all. Should you skip the planting, delay it, or plant elsewhere? To decide, ask yourself these questions:

- Is there a possible fix, such as a quick pass with the rototiller or wheelhoe?
- Are other crops doing well enough and are the safety factors high enough that you can afford to skip this planting?
- Which is a bigger risk: planting in the same spot (and having lower germination rates and high weed pressure) or planting somewhere else (and upsetting your long-term rotation)?
- If you have to plant in this seedbed with current poor conditions, should you expect lower yields?
- If you delay planting to improve the seedbed, is another variety with shorter DTM available for you to use?

Weather challenges

In every season there are times when the fields are wet, the air is cold and you wonder whether you should still plant. If you go ahead, you could cause soil compaction, undue stress to your plants, and discomfort to you and your employees. Provided your greenhouse transplants are healthy and your other crops are on schedule it's often worth delaying a planting. If you can't, you can still choose a lower impact approach such as planting by hand rather than with a tractor transplanter, or finding an alternate site that's better drained.

Sometimes you can see bad weather coming. If it's sunny and dry and the 7-day forecast is calling for rain, now is the time to do next week's ground preparation and planting. Many crops will hold in the field even though they are seeded earlier than planned. Other crops, like lettuce, if planted too early will simply result in too many plantings maturing at once. These decisions aren't always easy.

Ferme Coopérative Tourne-Sol

Unexpected weather conditions

Crop failures

Sometimes a crop has been compromised due to weeds, soil conditions, or pests, and the time to replant has passed. What should you do? You can seed an emergency quick-growing crop like radishes or leafy greens to substitute in your CSA baskets. You will also have to decide whether to keep the initial crop. Is the little bit that can be harvested worth the amount of work you'll put into it? Will the weeds go to seed and create problems for you in future years? Sometimes it's better to till the crop in and sow a cover crop. You'll have more time to properly manage your other crops.

HAVING A SUCCESSFUL SEASON

Your crop plan helps you envision what you want your season to be like. Paying attention to how it unfolds and tweaking it as circumstances arise makes a growing season successful. Always record your actions and the changes you make through the season. Your records will help you improve your plan from year to year.

Sweet Meadow Farm

Maureen Bostock and Elizabeth Snyder, Balderson Ontario

Frost free:
late May to mid
September

Farm size:
5 acres in vegetables

Marketing:
farmers market,
grocery stores,
Ottawa Organics
distribution
network

Maureen and Elizabeth run Sweet Meadow Farm in Balderson, Ontario. They have 10 cultivated acres with 5 acres in vegetables and 5 in cover crops. A variety of marketing outlets allows them to spread the harvest workload throughout the week.

To keep track of the crops they sell to each outlet during the season, Maureen and Elizabeth record their sales in a receipt book. At the end of the season, they make use of computer spreadsheets and evaluate the sales data from each outlet for each crop. They are always surprised by where they made money. High priced items aren't always the most profitable. Selling high volumes of lower priced items usually has a big impact.

Maureen maintains a field history chart showing each field's plantings since it was first planted to vegetables. During the winter, she uses the chart to plan the following year's rotation. Along with their sales analysis and any new marketing ideas, Maureen reviews her farm journal for notes on crop performance and reasons for changes to the previous year's plan.

From all this information, Maureen and Elizabeth develop the plan for the next season. They decrease or increase the quantity of crops proportionally to changes in their marketing plan. They always add a few new crops to keep ahead of the game, as other growers adopt the current year's innovations.

10 ANALYZE CROP PROFITABILITY

RECORD KEEPING really pays off during the winter when you begin to analyze your data. A profit analysis of your harvest records will inform your assessment of your farm, affect your production system, and influence your prices.

There are two ways to look at harvest data: profitability in space and profitability in time. These can be analyzed independently or together. You can set profitability targets and see how you fare against them, compare crops to one another and revise your prices.

PROFITABILITY IN SPACE

A TRUE PROFITABILITY ANALYSIS WOULD BE: *[gross sales - expenses = profit].*
This calculation can take a lot of time to perform. The profitability analyzes in this step offer shortcuts to evaluating and comparing crops. They are based on the two resources most limited on the average farm: time and space.

An analysis of profitability in space shows you which crops take a lot of space for little return, and which crops are very profitable for the field area they use. It involves 3 steps:

■ Set targets (How much do you need to make from a particular crop to meet your sales target?)

■ Calculate yields and determine your actual profitability (How much did you actually make?)

■ Compare your target with your actual profitability. (Did you make what you needed to make? Did you fall short?)

USE PROFITABILITY IN SPACE TO:

- *compare and choose crop varieties*
- *target the crops where management should be improved*
- *guide you in pricing*
- *choose which crops to grow more or less of in future years*
- *reduce workforce needs*

If you only grow crops that have a low profitability in space you have to cultivate, fertilize, plant, irrigate and weed more land to earn a particular gross revenue than if you grow crops that are more profitable in space.

SET TARGETS

How much do you need to make from your cultivated growing space to meet your sales target (Step 1)?

You can express this in terms of dollars per area (acre or hectare) or dollars per unit bed length.

AIM FOR MORE THAN THE MINIMUM PROFITABILITY
The more space you have and the less intensively you plant, the lower your profitability target will be. If you are growing on areas less than 20 acres (8 ha), your target should range from $12,000/ acre ($30,000/ha) to a maximum of $40,000/acre ($100,000/ha) for a very intensive growing operation.

Profitability per area ($/ha or $/ac):

[Gross sales ÷ growing space = $/area]

Profitability per unit bed length:

[($/acre ÷ 43,560 sq ft/ac) * bed width (ft) = $/bedft]
or
[($/hectare ÷ 10,000 m²/ha) * bed width (m) = $/bedm]

Bruce and Hanna plan on grossing $24,000 this year .
They will have vegetables growing in 5 blocks of 1/6 acre (1/15ᵗʰ of a hectare).
[$24,000 ÷5/6 acre = $28,800/ac ($72,000/ha)]
[($28,800/acre ÷ 43,560 sq ft/ac) * 5 ft/bed = $3.31/bedft]
[($72,000/ha ÷ 10,000 m²/ha) *1.5 m/bed = $10.8/bedm]

Squash curing in the greenhouse

Ferme Coopérative Tourne-Sol

CALCULATE YIELDS AND DETERMINE YOUR PROFITABILITY

How much did your crops actually yield? You may find it useful to compare this with the estimated yields you used in step 3.

Crop Harvested:

The total amount you harvested over the whole season (how many bunches, kg, etc.)

Bed Length Harvested:

The total bed length harvested over the whole season (how many bed meters or bed feet)

Yield:

The amount of crop per unit row length you harvested. (how many bunches of carrots / rowfoot, kg of tomatoes / rowmeter, etc.)
[Crop Harvested ÷ (bed length harvested * rows/bed) = yield]

Your **actual profitability in space** will vary from year to year. It can be expressed in terms of unit bed length or in terms of area.

Profitability per unit bed length ($/bedm or $/bedft):

[(Yield ÷ rows/bed) * unit price = $/unit bed length]

Profitability per area ($/ha or $/ac):

[($/bedft ÷ bedwidth (ft)) * 43,560 sq ft /ac = $ /ac]
Or
[($/bedm ÷ bedwidth (m)) * 10,000 m² /ha = $/ha]

Some of Bruce and Hanna's harvest data (all on 5 ft wide beds):
- *First Lady Tomato: 616 lbs for 200 bedft with 1 row*
- *Big Beef Tomato: 820 lbs for 200 bedft with 1 row*
- *Carrots: 2310 bunches of carrots for 1050 bedft with 3 rows*
- *Peas: 220 lbs for 500 bedft with 1 row*

They are thinking about adding Butternut squash to their garden next year. Their neighbour harvested 120 squashes off of 130 bedft with 1 row (6 ft wide beds).

*Bruce and Hanna calculate their crop yields and profitability.
This is how they did it for First Lady Tomatoes:*

Calculate yield:
*[616 lbs ÷ (200 bedm * 1 row/bed) = 3.08 lbs / row ft]*

Calculate profitability per bed length ($/bedft):
*[(3.08 lbs/row ft ÷ 1 row/bed) * $2/lb = $6.16 / bedft]*

Calculate profitability per area ($/ac):
*[($6.16/bedft ÷ 5 ft) * 43,560 sqft/acre = $53,665/acre]*

Bruce and Hanna will never actually make $47,916 growing carrots. Nor do they grow one acre of carrots. In fact, they probably wouldn't be able to sell one acre of carrots at $2.50/ bunch. Dollars per acre is simply a tool for comparison.

This table summarises the results for a few crops:

CROP	PRICE	YIELD	$ / BEDFT	$ /ACRE
First Lady Tomato	$2.00 / lb	3.08 lbs / row ft	$6.16	$53,665
Big Beef Tomato	$2.00 / lb	4.1 lbs / row ft	$8.20	$71,438
Carrots	$2.50 / bunch	0.73 bunches / row ft	$5.50	$47,916
Peas	$5.50 / lb	0.44 lbs / row ft	$2.42	$21,083
Butternut Squash	$4.00 / fruit	0.92 fruits / row ft	$3.69	$26,806

COMPARE YOUR TARGET WITH YOUR ACTUAL PROFITABILITY

- Rank your crops from most profitable to least.
- Check whether your crops meet your profitability targets. As long as you have several vegetables that exceed your targets, you can offset your lower-profit crops. If most of your crops don't meet your targets, you will be unable to meet your gross sales targets.
- Pay attention to the crops with low profitability in space. Any reason you uncover for their low profitability will help you improve your results in the future.
- Consider the total area devoted to each crop you grow. If you raise profitability of the crops that take the most space in your field, it will have the greatest impact on your overall profitability.

AFTER YOU'VE DONE YOUR COMPARISON, ASK YOURSELF THESE QUESTIONS:

- *Were yields lower than normal?*
- *Can yields be increased?*
- *Could spacing be changed?*

- *Could the price be increased?*
- *Does this crop draw clients to the market stall?*

- *Is this crop available at a key moment in the season (early/late)?*

Bruce and Hanna's target is $3.31/bedft ($28,800/acre). Peas ($21,083/acre) and their potential squash crop ($26,806/acre) don't meet their target. These are the crops they focus on.

Peas:
- *Yields were average, but perhaps they could be increased by switching from dwarf to climbing varieties.*
- *Spacing is difficult to change.*
- *At $5.50/lb, Bruce and Hanna would rather not raise the price but they might have to if yields don't increase.*
- *Peas are ready early in the year and help fill CSA baskets.*

Squash:
- *This price – $4/fruit – is already high compared to other farms' prices.*
- *They can change spacing from 6 ft wide beds to 5 ft wide beds. If they had the same yield, profitability would increase to $32,167/acre.*
- *They will keep careful yield records to see if certain varieties yield better than others.*

Bruce and Hanna also compare different tomato varieties. They notice First Lady didn't yield as much as Big Beef. They could grow more Big Beef tomatoes and less First Lady to increase the profitability of their tomato crop. However, Big Beef and First Lady aren't equivalent in terms of their DTM, shape, size and taste. They don't know if their clients will like Big Beef as much as First Lady.

PROFITABILITY IN TIME

At some farms, space is more limited than at others. But surplus time is in short supply everywhere. That's why it's useful to analyze profitability in time. It allows you to critically evaluate your harvesting techniques. If a crop brings a mediocre financial return and takes forever to harvest, process, and package, it has a low profitability in time. Identifying the crops that are not profitable in time helps improve your farm management.

To analyze profitability in time:
- ■ Set your profitability targets
- ■ Calculate your actual profitability
- ■ Compare your profitability to your targets

SET PROFITABILITY TARGETS

Calculate how many hours are worked on your farm

Estimate the number of hours each person on the farm (owners and employees) works during the year. Two thousand hours is a good estimate for a full time farmer. Add up the hours each person works. This is the total number of available hours on your farm per year.

Figure out how the time is spent

At the end of the day, we often don't know where time has gone. Roughly speaking, at La Ferme Coopérative Tourne-Sol the total work time throughout the year is divided more or less equally among the following (20% each):

- crop establishment (greenhouse, seeding, transplanting)
- crop management (weeding, fertilizing, controlling insects, staking, etc.)
- harvesting, washing, packing
- marketing and selling
- administration, planning, and maintenance

You can use this approximation for your own farm.

Calculate a target hourly rate

WHAT IS A REASONABLE HOURLY ($/HR) TARGET? *When you first start farming, you can probably expect to average $40 to $60 an hour for most crops. With harvesting experience and good wash station design, you can probably raise your average to $70 to $100 an hour for most crops. Refining your harvest techniques will help you meet your targets and free up time to perform other tasks and operations.*

Although you are busy when you plan, plant or weed, you only generate revenue when you market and sell. This means you have to make 100% of your sales in 20% of your time. Similarly, you have to harvest 100% of the crops you will sell in 20% of your time.

[Gross Sales ÷ (Total Hours ÷ 5) = target $/hr]

Hanna and Bruce each work about 2000 hours per year. They have no employees. Their total number of work hours is 4000 hours. Their gross sales target for the first year is $28,000.

[$28,000 ÷ (4000 hours ÷ 5) = $35/hr]

They want to increase gross sales in future years and would like to work about the same amount in the future. They set a $40,000 future gross sales target.

[$40,000 ÷ (4000 hours ÷ 5) = $50/hr]

To meet their current sales targets, the time Bruce and Hanna spend harvesting has to be worth $35/hour. If they harvest faster – at a rate worth $50/hr – it would be enough to meet their future targets.

CALCULATE YOUR ACTUAL PROFITABILITY IN TIME

You can calculate your profitability occasionally during the season.

- Record how long it takes to harvest, wash and pack a certain crop.
- Write down how many units were harvested and processed during that time.
- Calculate your profitability using this equation:

[Units harvested * $/unit ÷ harvest time = actual $/hr]

It took Bruce and Hanna 1.5 hours to harvest and process 54 bunches of carrots (3 hours total). It also took them half an hour (1 hour total) to harvest 7 lbs of sugar snap peas.

*[54 carrot bunches * $2.50/bunch ÷ 3 hours = $45/hour]*

*[7 lbs of peas * $5.50/lb ÷ 1 hour = $38.50/hr]*

COMPARE YOUR ACTUAL PROFITABILITY TO YOUR TARGETS

CROP FAILURES
Don't rush to drop a crop that doesn't do as well as it should. Be on the lookout for plantings that succumbed to weather, pests, weeds or something else. These are crop failures, and you can counter them by improving your everyday farm management. If a crop does poorly year after year, it is probably not the right match for you.

Analyzing profitability in time helps you to identify the crops that would benefit most from changes in your harvesting, washing, or packaging technique. Modify your harvest techniques and see if you can raise your profitability in time. Keep records of your efficiency for certain key crops to see how it evolves over the season or over the course of several years.

Remember that your profitability in time is an average value. Crops that are ready for harvest quickly will offset crops that take a long time.

Bruce and Hanna realize that their (harvest) profitability for peas and carrots is adequate for their current financial targets, but their harvest techniques need to be improved if they are going to meet their future sales ambitions. They brainstorm ways to increase harvest efficiency for peas, which have a lower profitability in time. Hanna wonders if different varieties might be more productive and faster to harvest. They also decide to abandon plantings sooner when productivity drops. They realise that trying to find the last peas left in the planting really slows them down. They also decide to have a pea picking competition between the two of them. The one who harvests the most peas will get a special treat.

COMPARE PROFITABILITY IN SPACE AND TIME

Some crops are profitable in space but not in time or vice versa. Not all your crops have to meet both targets. It is okay to grow a crop that is less profitable in space or in time, if you also grow crops that are more profitable. They will balance each other out.

What about crops that meet neither target? Should you stop producing them? That depends. Do these crops provide diversity at a time of year where few things are ready to harvest? Do they draw additional clients to your stall? Do you love growing them? It's important to balance your crop profitability with these other concerns. Sometimes, the added benefits do not offset the profit loss. In these cases, you may want to drop that crop from your crop plan. If you want to grow something that you are obviously losing money on, consider growing less of it.

Bruce and Hanna see that the profitability of their sugar snap peas is significantly lower than both their space and time profitability targets. But peas help fill their early CSA shares. They choose to keep them in the crop plan. If they found other crops to grow for their early shares, they would stop producing peas.

REVIEW YOUR PRICES

Your prices are a key element in crop profitability. If a crop yields well, but is still below your targets, look at your pricing. Raising your prices will increase your profit.

Should you feel bad about raising your prices? When people buy your vegetables, they are buying more than just water and vitamins. They are also buying your time and the expertise that you have invested to grow them. Don't be afraid to raise your prices if you need to. If you develop a relationship with your clientele based on fresh, high quality, organic produce that tastes great, your clients will be lining up at your stall.

Bruce and Hanna realize that peas fall short both in terms of profitability in time and profitability in space and decide to raise their price next year. They figure that with the same yields, raising the price from $5.50/lb to $6.50/lb will boost productivity in space to $24,916/acre and productivity in time to $45.50/hr. These values are closer to their targets.

NORTHBROOK FARM

HEATHER STRETCH, SAANICHTON, BRITISH COLUMBIA

FROST FREE:
mid May to late
October

FARM SIZE:
20 acres; 5 acres
in vegetables and
blueberries

MARKETING:
vegetable box
program, 2
farmers markets,
restaurants and
grocery stores

HEATHER began her organic farm on Vancouver Island in 2001. She now has 2.5 acres in vegetables and 2.5 acres in blueberries. Of the remaining 15 acres, parts are fallowed, and parts are rented to other small growers.

To address marketing challenges, Heather bought and expanded Saanich Organics, a small organic vegetable marketing business, teaming up with two other local farmers. Together they could increase the diversity and quantity of produce they had to offer to retail and market customers in Victoria. Besides raising three children, Heather works part of her time on the farm and part managing the marketing business.

Every Tuesday and Friday, the farmers who produce for Saanichton Organics call her before noon to tell her what they will harvest. She compiles the list of available produce, determines the content of the vegetable box for home deliveries, and calls the 20-25 chefs on her distribution route, aiming to sell everything else.

Although they market their produce together, the three farms plan and manage their crops independently. Nonetheless, if Heather wanted to grow a new crop, she would discuss it with the two other farmers.

In January, Heather devotes about a week to crop planning. She starts by reflecting on the previous season. For each crop she considers how well it grew, how much she enjoyed growing it, and whether she could have sold more.

She then compiles her sales data in a spreadsheet and calculates how much money she made from each crop. This value divided by the number of beds grown for each crop gives a gross income per bed ratio with which she can rank and compare crops.

Heather aims for an average of $400 per bed ($1 per square foot, or $4 per bedfoot). Profitable crops gross $600 or more per bed. Some crops, such as melons, squash and peas fall below these targets. She continues to grow these however, because she enjoys it and wants to provide diversity for chefs and for the box program.

Heather's basic unit for crop planning is one 4' x 100' bed. She prefers to grow whole beds of a crop or variety to simplify planning, data analysis and record keeping. After analysing her data, she chooses which crops and how many beds of each to grow. She then completes her field map.

Rather than use an established crop rotation, Heather follows these guiding principles:

- Each crop family goes where it hasn't been for the longest time possible.
- Cucurbits are placed first since 1/3 of the beds are cucurbits.
- She places pastured chickens in a fallow area.
- Last year's chicken beds get a buckwheat cover crop. The buckwheat is tilled under in July then seeded to root crops (carrots, parsnips, beets, winter radish, rutabaga).
- She places Kale and Swiss chard (8 beds), and corn.
- Last, she fits the remaining crops (mostly shallow-rooted greens and pea shoots) here and there in any leftover beds.

Heather often runs out of space at the last step, and has to decide what to grow and what to drop. Her profitability analyzes make these decisions easier. She feels it is important to resist the temptation to increase the cropped area, instead trying to grow more efficiently in the same space.

NORTHBROOK FARM
HEATHER STRETCH, SAANICHTON, BRITISH COLUMBIA

11 PLAN FOR NEXT YEAR

W INTER IS THE PERFECT TIME to review your growing season with everyone involved in the farm's management. Use your records, notes, memories and profitability analyzes to evaluate how successful your crop plan was out in the field, and decide what you would like to change. How will your next crop plan differ? Let's go through each of the steps one by one and see.

Ferme Coopérative Tourne-Sol

Time to plan

STEP 1 – REVIEW YOUR FINANCIAL GOALS

- Can you produce more vegetables and raise your farm gross sales?
- Did you meet your salary goals? Were they adequate for your personal financial needs?
- Can you maintain or lower expenses?

If you raise your farm income and lower your farm expenses it will lead to more money in your pocket.

STEP 2 — REVIEW YOUR MARKETING PLAN

- Did you meet your sales targets?
- Were your clients pleased with the diversity, quantity and quality of your produce?
- How did the value of your CSA shares compare with their price? Could you raise your share price?
- What is the potential for your distribution outlets to expand? Did your market stand sales plateau, or are they still increasing? Could you add additional weeks to your CSA?
- Can you change your crop mix towards crops that proved more profitable, as explained in step 10?

STEP 3 — REVIEW YOUR PLANTING SCHEDULE

Compare your *harvest records* with your *field worksheets.* How did your *planned* harvest dates differ from your *actual* harvest dates? You can offset the discrepancy by choosing a different variety. In some cases changing **field dates** will have the biggest impact.

Consider whether you could extend the season for certain key vegetables. Row covers and unheated tunnels allow you to thwart frost dates in the spring and fall. If you have the growing space, you can plant hardy crops (like lettuce, peas, or carrots) especially early to get a jump start at market. If you lose the crops, you can replant the beds. In each case, choose varieties that are adapted to the cold.

Adjust **yield** estimates carefully. Compare the yields you used in step 3 with your season's actual yields (step 10).

- Are there any unfavourable circumstances that explain why your actual yields were lower than your planned yields? If not, consider lowering your planning yields or raising your SF.
- Were your actual yields higher than your planned yields? If so, do not immediately raise your planning yields. Each season is different and will affect crops differently. Wait until you've had the same yield for a few years before you adjust your planning yields.

- Adjust your **field SF** as you observe how predictable each crop is to grow and as you determine how easily you can sell any surplus. A crop like kale, for example, which matures on time and holds well in the fields, might only need a SF of 1.1. Broccoli on the other hand, which matures over a number of days and is popular with clients, should have a SF of 1.3.

Step 4 – review your crop maps

How did the combination and location of crops in your field blocks work out?
- Were your reasons for grouping crops together sound?
- Was management (planting, irrigation, row cover, harvest, incorporation) helped or hindered by the mix of crops in each block?
- Were there any serious pest or disease outbreaks that will have an impact on your crop rotation?
- Have you discovered any areas in your field – compacted soil or poor drainage, for example – that require special management?

Over time you can develop a rotation in which the content of each field block stays constant, but is tailored to your field needs and distribution methods.

Step 5 – review your crop variety selection

Evaluate your varieties based on their market appeal (taste, flavour, colour and storage ability) and your production needs (pest and disease resistance, DTMs, and seasonality).
- Did your standard varieties meet your objectives?
- Did any of your trialed varieties stand out, and are they worth growing in larger quantities?
- What needs are you trying to meet with next year's variety trials?

STEP 6 — REVIEW YOUR GREENHOUSE SCHEDULE

GH Dates:
- Was your GH schedule in sync with your field schedule?
- Were seedlings ready when they left the greenhouse?
- Would adjusting the **GH days** of problem crops produce better seedlings?

Tray size:
If you plant into trays with more cells you won't need as much greenhouse space. Use smaller cells cautiously though; they dry out more quickly and don't allow plants to hold very long.

GH SF:
Don't adjust your greenhouse safety factors too much. Crop losses are more frequent in the greenhouse than in the field.

STEP 7 — REVIEW YOUR SEED ORDER

- Did you run out of seed? If so, recalibrate your seeder more precisely, or adjust the seeds/gram value.
- Were you satisfied with the quality of the seeds you received? Did a particular company have consistently high or low seed quality?

STEP 8 — REVIEW YOUR FIELD OPERATIONS CALENDAR

- Was your seedbed deep and fine enough?
- Do you need to modify your ground preparation sequence?
- Can you reduce tillage while still preparing a nice seedbed?
- Were cover crops adequately decomposed when you planted?

STEP 9 – REVIEW HOW YOU CARRIED OUT YOUR CROP PLAN

How accurately did your crop plan predict your actual season? If you had to adjust your crop plan, what was the reason? Was it:

- An error in your planning assumptions in steps 3 to 8?
- Due to weather or timing? Regularly walking your fields to observe your crops, weeds, and soil, and carefully compiling your to-do lists with an eye on the weather, can help you prioritize.
- Because there was more work than your farm team could handle? Hiring help, or taking on apprentices increases the amount you can do, but it also has an impact on your financial goals.

Did you manage to keep good records? Were they helpful as you reviewed your season? Adapt your record keeping to fill any knowledge gaps.

Now you are ready to go back to step 1 and set your goals for the coming year.

ORCHARD HILL FARM

KEN AND MARTHA LAING, SPARTA, ONTARIO.

FROST FREE:
early May to mid October

FARM SIZE:
80 acres; 5 acres in vegetables; 9 acres in cover crops

MARKETING:
167 share CSA

ORCHARD HILL FARM is north of Lake Erie on land that had been in Martha's family for six generations. Their ecological and social values brought Ken and Martha to farming in 1979, and continue to direct their decisions. They use Suffolk Punch draft horses to reduce their use of fossil fuels and to complete fertility cycles.

They began their CSA in 1997 with 25 shares, to generate a university fund for their daughter Ellen's education. Over the next years, the Laings discovered they preferred the financial stability of a CSA to their previous crops and marketing methods – mainly grain cash crops, and pick-your-own small fruits. Now the main focus of the farm, they hope to have 200 CSA shares by 2011.

The CSA runs from early May to mid-October. Their 6B climatic zone helps them get into the fields in early April, but Ken and Martha depend on four unheated tunnels, row cover, and perennials such as asparagus and rhubarb to provide early variety and abundance for their shares. Strawberries help transition the crop mix into the summer bounty of vegetables.

Seedlings are started in a 15' x 20' greenhouse and a 4' x 16' hot bed, then transplanted by hand. Direct seeding is done with a push seeder. Horse drawn implements are the principal means of cultivation and soil preparation, with some help from hoes and wheel hoes. Most rows are spaced 36" apart to accommodate the horses. The exceptions are head lettuce and salad greens which are planted in 4 rows over a 36" growing space.

The 80 acre farm includes pasture, hay fields and grain crops for the horses. The vegetable garden is divided into three areas with different crop rotations.

■ 3 acres in annual vegetables and strawberries plus 9 acres in cover crop
  » Year 1: Vegetables and strawberries
  » Years 2 and 3: Hay (cut and left on the field to build fertility)
  » Year 4: Buckwheat and rye to clean up weeds before returning to year 1

This rotation increases soil fertility and reduces weeds on a large land base while effectively breaking weed and disease cycles.

- 1.5 acres in a trial high fertility rotation
  - » Year 1: Sweet corn (compost applied before)
  - » Year 2: Potatoes
  - » Year 3: Squash (heavily mulched for weed control and fertility)

  This rotation is designed to test Ken's theory that Colorado potato beetle pressure is reduced in high fertility situations. They are still evaluating the results after completing the first rotation cycle.

- 0.5 acres in perennial crops: rhubarb, asparagus and raspberries.

During the growing season Martha keeps records in a field notebook and a greenhouse notebook. She records varieties, planting dates, locations, and the amount planted (rowfeet, number of plants or number of trays), plus other garden or greenhouse tasks and any observations.

Ken and Martha start planning in late summer for the following year. They determine the number of shares they'll have based on their budget and expansion plans. For instance, going from 167 to 185 shares represents a 7.2% increase, thus they would grow 7.2% more of each crop. Then they determine if they have enough land prepared for next year, and whether they could grow additional crops by double cropping after early crops.

The next planning phase occurs over a couple weeks in January. Martha reviews her notebooks to see how many rowfeet of each vegetable they grew. For each crop, she adjusts the rowfeet according to its performance for current needs and the percentage change in the number of CSA shares for the next year. The new area is finally adjusted for standard field dimensions. For example:

> If 600 rowft of beets had not been enough for 167 shares last year, she might raise it to 700 rowft for the coming year. Then, since the number of shares is increasing to 185, Martha would increase 700 rowft by 7.2% to 750ft. This could be rounded to 800 rowft (4 x 200ft rows).

Martha stresses that an important part of planning is getting soil tests, knowing what micronutrients crops need, and making sure to prepare the soil in advance. "It's hard to grow good vegetables on bad land," she says.

CONCLUSION

THE ULTIMATE GOAL OF A CROP PLAN is to ensure your farm provides a decent and comfortable living for you and your workers while promoting ecological biodiversity and nurturing your soil.

As you strive for this goal, your crop planning will become more intuitive. You will learn how much you can grow and which crops you enjoy producing the most. You will also carve out a solid niche for yourself and get better at predicting what you should produce to satisfy your buyers' demands. The analysis you do of your records will provide you with precise yield estimates and safety factors that reflect your methods of production and give you a good idea of how profitable each crop is.

Your crop planning, however, will always begin with setting your goals and then walking through the steps to achieve them.

As a final word, we suggest you apply the steps proposed in this book as carefully as you can, and modify and adapt them to suit your needs as you gain experience. Above all, farming and crop planning should remain fun and exciting. Good luck!

A VEGETABLE REFERENCE CHARTS

THESE REFERENCE CHARTS contain basic information useful for all 11 steps of this book. This information has been compiled from our personal experience, the experience of other farmers, farming books, and seed catalogues. All the columns in each chart will be explained in the step where they are used. These charts are recommendations, and are not meant to replace any farm management practices and information that work on your farm.

Crops can be direct seeded (DS) into the ground, or started in a greenhouse or nursery bed, and transplanted (TP) to the field. Though the reference charts present most crops as either DS or TP, many crops can be planted either way. Both methods have advantages and disadvantages.

	TRANSPLANTED CROPS (TP)	DIRECT SEEDED CROPS (DS)
ADVANTAGES	■ Head start over weeds. Reduces the amount of weeding. ■ Ready to harvest quicker. ■ Easier to replant the area to another crop or cover crop. ■ For some vegetables, the only way to guarantee it will reach maturity.	■ Do not need a greenhouse. ■ Very quick to seed with a seeder. ■ Easy to seed an unplanned row, (no worry about not having seedlings ready in the GH, simply grab some seed and head to the field).
DISADVANTAGES	■ Need to produce seedlings or buy them. ■ Transplanting takes time.	■ Germination can be a problem. ■ Vital to control weed pressure.

CHART A1 – DIRECT SEEDED CROP REFERENCE CHART

CROP	FAMILY	DTM [*a]	PLANTING FREQUENCY	ROWS PER BED	SEEDING RATE SEEDS PER FT	SEEDS PER M
Beans	Legumes	56	2 – 4 weeks	2	12	35
Beets bunched	Chenopods	49	2 – 4 weeks	3	16	50
Beets topped	Chenopods	49	2 – 4 weeks	3	16	50
Brassica Greens	Brassica	28	1 – 2 weeks	3	55	180
Carrots bunched	Umbel	56	2 – 4 weeks	3	30	100
Carrots topped	Umbel	56	2 – 4 weeks	3	30	100
Cilantro	Umbel	56	1 – 2 weeks	3	30	100
Corn	Graminae	70	2 weeks	2	2	7
Cucumbers	Cucurbits	63	4 weeks	1	3 [*b]	10 [*b]
Dill	Umbel	49	1 – 2 weeks	3	30	100
Garlic	Alliums	*d	once	3	2	7
Lettuce	Composite	28	1 – 2 weeks	3	55	180
Melons	Cucurbits	84	4 weeks	1	2 [*c]	7 [*c]
Parsnip	Umbel	112	once	3	20	70
Peas	Legumes	49	once	1 to 2	25	80
Potatoes	Solanacea	70	once	1 to 2	1	3
Radish, spring	Brassica	28	1 – 2 weeks	3	30	100
Radish, winter	Brassica	49	2 – 4 weeks	3	6	20
Spinach large leaf	Chenopods	42	2 – 4 weeks	3	10	33
Squash, summer	Cucurbits	49	4 weeks	1	3 [*b]	10 [*b]
Squash, winter	Cucurbits	98	4 weeks	1	2 [*c]	7 [*c]
Turnip	Brassica	42	2 – 4 weeks	3	30	100

a: DTM have to be multiples of 7 for the formulas in this book to be synchronized
b: thin to 1 plant every 30 cm (12")
c: thin to 1 plant every 45 cm (18")
d: plant garlic in fall, harvest in mid July to early August

| CROP | YIELD | | POTENTIAL | SEEDS PER |
	PER ROW FOOT	PER ROW METER	PROFITABILITY PER ACRE	GRAM
Beans	0.55 lb	0.8 kg	low	4.2
Beets bunched	0.5 bunch	1.7 bunches	medium	55
Beets topped	1.1 lb	1.7 kg	medium	55
Brassica Greens	0.55 lb	0.8 kg	high	450
Carrots bunched	0.5 bunch	1.7 bunches	medium	640
Carrots topped	1 lb	1.7 kg	medium	640
Cilantro	1 bunch	3.3 bunches	high	75
Corn	2 ears	6.7 ears	low	5.5
Cucumbers	5 fruit	16.7 fruit	low	38
Dill	1 bunch	3.3 bunches	high	400
Garlic	2 heads	6.7 heads	medium	varies
Lettuce	0.4 lb	0.7 kg	high	800
Melons	0.75 fruit	2.5 fruit	low	40
Parsnip	0.4 lb	0.7 kg	low	220
Peas	0.2 lb	0.3 kg	low	4.5
Potatoes	2.5 lb	4 kg	low	varies
Radish, spring	1 bunch	3.3 bunches	medium	90
Radish, winter	2 roots	6.7 roots	medium	56
Spinach large leaf	0.35 lb	0.5 kg	high	80
Squash, summer	6 fruit	20 fruit	medium	6 – 10
Squash, winter	1 fruit	3.3 fruit	low	6 – 15
Turnip	0.7 bunch	2.3 bunches	medium	390

Information adapted from Johnny's Selected Seeds Catalog
and la Ferme Coopérative Tourne-Sol farm records

CHART A2 – TRANSPLANTED CROP REFERENCE CHART

CROP	FAMILY	DTM	PLANTING FREQUENCY	ROWS PER BED	INROW SPACING FT	M	YIELD PER ROW FOOT	PER ROW METER
Basil	Labiatea	63	2 – 4 weeks	3	1	0.3	1 plant	3.3 plants
Broccoli	Brassica	49	2 – 4 weeks	2	1.5	0.45	0.67 heads	2.2 heads
Brussel Sprouts	Brassica	91	once	2	2	0.6	0.5 stalks	1.7 stalks
Cabbage, storage	Brassica	91	2 – 4 weeks	2	1.5	0.45	0.67 heads	2.2 heads
Cabbage, summer	Brassica	63	2 – 4 weeks	2	1.5	0.45	0.67 heads	2.2 heads
Cauliflower	Brassica	49	2 – 4 weeks	2	1.5	0.45	0.67 heads	2.2 heads
Celeriac	Umbel	98	once	3	1	0.3	1 roots	3.3 roots
Celery	Umbel	84	once	3	1	0.3	1 heads	3.3 heads
Chard	Chenopods	42	2 – 4 weeks	3	1	0.3	1.5 bunches	5 bunches
Chinese Cabbage	Brassica	49	2 – 4 weeks	3	1.5	0.45	0.67 fruit	2.2 fruit
Corn	Graminae	56	2 weeks	2	0.5	0.15	2 ears	6.6 ears
Cucumbers	Cucurbits	49	4 weeks	1	1.5	0.45	4 fruit	13 fruit
Eggplant	Solanacea	63	once	2	1.5	0.45	1.1 lbs	1.7 kg
Fennel	Umbel	63	2 – 4 weeks	3	1	0.3	1 heads	3.3 heads
Kale	Brassica	42	2 – 4 weeks	3	1	0.3	1.5 bunches	5 bunches
Kohlrabi	Brassica	28	2 – 4 weeks	3	1	0.3	1 heads	3.3 heads
Leeks	Alliums	77	once	3	*a	*a	1 bunch	3.3 bunches
Lettuce	Aster	35	1 – 3 weeks	3	1	0.3	1 heads	3.3 heads
Melons	Cucurbits	70	4 weeks	1	1.5	0.45	0.75 fruit	2.5 fruit
Onions	Alliums	91	once	3	*a	*a	1.5 lbs	2.2 kg
Parsley	Umbel	70	4 weeks	3	1	0.3	1.5 bunches	5 bunches
Pepper	Solanacea	70	once	2	1.5	0.45	2 fruit	7 fruit
Rutabaga	Brassica	77	4 weeks	3	1	0.3	1 roots	3.3 roots
Scallions	Alliums	63	2 – 4 weeks	3	*b	*b	2 bunches	6.6 bunches
Squash, summer	Cucurbits	42	4 weeks	1	1.5	0.45	6 fruit	20 fruit
Squash, winter	Cucurbits	84	4 weeks	1	2	0.6	1 fruit	3.3 fruit
Tomato	Solanacea	63	once	1	1.5	0.45	2.2 lbs	3.3 kg

a: planted every 10 cm (4 inches) or 3 plants every 30 cm (12")

b: planted every 5 cm (2 inches) or 6 plants every 30 cm (12")

c: plant 1 seed/cell or in open flat then pot up to larger size cell

d: tray size to pot up to

CROP	POTENTIAL PROFITABILITY PER ACRE	GREENHOUSE DAYS	TRAY SIZE	SEEDS PER CELL	SEEDS PER GRAM
Basil	high	28 – 42	72	2	560
Broccoli	low	28 – 42	72	2	220
Brussel Sprouts	low	28 – 42	72	2	250
Cabbage, storage	low	28 – 42	72	2	250
Cabbage, summer	low	28 – 42	72	2	250
Cauliflower	low	28 – 42	72	2	285
Celeriac	medium	84	72^{*d}	PU^{*c}	2400
Celery	medium	84	72^{*d}	PU^{*c}	2400
Chard	high	35 – 42	72	1	65
Chinese Cabbage	low	28 – 42	72	2	330
Corn	low	14	50	2	5.5
Cucumbers	low	21	24	2	38
Eggplant	medium	56	50^{*d}	PU^{*c}	220
Fennel	medium	35 – 42	72	2	250
Kale	high	28 – 42	72	2	250
Kohlrabi	medium	28 – 42	72	2	230
Leeks	medium	56	72	3a	350
Lettuce	medium	28 – 42	72	3	800
Melons	low	21	24	2	40
Onions	medium	56	72	3a	230
Parsley	high	42	72	3	500
Pepper	medium	63	50^{*d}	PU^{*c}	140
Rutabaga	medium	28 – 42	72	2	330
Scallions	high	56	72	6^{*b}	450
Squash, summer	medium	21	24	2	6 – 10
Squash, winter	low	21	24	2	6 – 15
Tomato	medium	42	50^{*d}	PU^{*c}	350

Information adapted from Johnny's Selected Seeds Catalog
and la Ferme Coopérative Tourne-Sol farm records

CHART A3 – CROP PLANTING AND HARVEST PERIODS

FAMILY	CROP	PLANTING PERIODS †			LAST SUCCESSION PLANTING DATE
		HARDIEST CROPS	HARDY CROPS	FROST SENSITIVE CROPS	
Alliums	Garlic	Garlic: plant in mid Oct – mid Nov			
Alliums	Leeks		■		
Alliums	Onions		■		
Alliums	Scallions	■	■		Aug 1
Aster	Lettuce	■	■		Mid Aug
Brassica	Brassica Greens	■	■		Mid Sept
Brassica	Broccoli		■		Aug 1
Brassica	Brussel Sprouts		■		
Brassica	Cabbage		■		Aug 1
Brassica	Cauliflower		■		Aug 1
Brassica	Chinese Cabbage		■		Mid Aug
Brassica	Kale	■	■		Mid Aug
Brassica	Kohlrabi		■		Mid Aug
Brassica	Radish Spring	■	■		Sept 1
Brassica	Radish Winter		■		Mid Aug
Brassica	Rutabaga		■		Mid July
Brassica	Turnip		■		Mid Aug
Chenopods	Beets	■	■		Aug 1
Chenopods	Chard	■	■		Mid Aug
Chenopods	Spinach	■	■		Sept 1
Cucurbits	Cucumbers			■	Mid July
Cucurbits	Melons			■	
Cucurbits	Squash Summer			■	Mid July
Cucurbits	Squash Winter			■	
Fab	Beans			■	Aug 1
Fab	Peas	■	■		
Graminae	Corn			■	
Solanacea	Eggplant			■	
Solanacea	Pepper			■	
Solanacea	Potatoes		■		
Solanacea	Tomato			■	
Umbel	Carrots	■	■		Aug 1
Umbel	Celeriac			■	
Umbel	Celery			■	
Umbel	Dill/Cilantro	■	■		Sept 1
Umbel	Fennel		■	■	Aug 1
Umbel	Parsley		■		Aug 1
Umbel	Parsnip	■	■		

† **Shaded areas** represent window of opportunity to plant crop:
Hardiest crops: Plant as soon as ground is workable (resists heavy frost). **Hardy Crops:** Plant after last chance of heavy frost (resists light frost). **Frost Sensitive Crops:** Plant after last frost date. **Last succession planting date:** based on daylight availability for most of agricultural Canada. Some climatic zones may need crop protection from frost and snow using row cover or tunnels.

CROP	JUNE	JULY	AUG	SEPT	AFTER KILLING FROST	UNTIL HEAVIEST FROST AND SNOW
CROP AVAILABILITY PERIODS ††						
Garlic			▓	*	*	*
Leeks				▓	▓	▓
Onions			▓	▓	*	*
Scallions	▓	▓	▓	▓	▓	▓
Lettuce	▓	▓	▓	▓	▓	
Brassica Greens	▓	▓	▓	▓	▓	▓
Broccoli	▓	▓	▓	▓	▓	
Brussel Sprouts				▓	▓	▓
Cabbage		▓	▓	▓	▓	
Cauliflower		▓	▓	▓	▓	
Chinese Cabbage			▓	▓	▓	*
Kale	▓	▓	▓	▓	▓	▓
Kohlrabi	▓	▓	▓	▓	▓	*
Radish Spring	▓	▓	▓	▓	▓	
Radish Winter			▓	▓	▓	*
Rutabaga		▓	▓	▓	▓	*
Turnip	▓	▓	▓	▓	▓	*
Beets	▓	▓	▓	▓	▓	
Chard	▓	▓	▓	▓	▓	
Spinach	▓	▓	▓	▓	▓	▓
Cucumbers		▓	▓	▓		
Melons		▓	▓	▓		
Squash Summer		▓	▓	▓		
Squash Winter				▓	*	*
Beans		▓	▓	▓		
Peas	▓	▓				
Corn		▓	▓	▓		
Eggplant		▓	▓	▓		
Pepper		▓	▓	▓		
Potatoes		▓	▓	▓	*	*
Tomato		▓	▓	▓		
Carrots		▓	▓	▓	▓	
Celeriac			▓	▓	▓	*
Celery			▓	▓	▓	
Dill/Cilantro	▓	▓	▓	▓	▓	
Fennel			▓	▓	▓	
Parsley	▓	▓	▓	▓	▓	▓
Parsnip				▓	▓	▓

†† **Shaded areas** represent availability of crops either fresh from the field or as storage vegetables.

* **Crop** held in storage.

APPENDIX

B FIELD LAYOUT

L AYING OUT YOUR FIELDS in a simple, structured and modular manner will help you manage your farm. This appendix includes step-by-step instructions on how to divide your fields into manageable blocks containing a standard amount of growing space.

Standardizing your field layout should facilitate crop rotation design, allow for easier yield comparison between areas, and permit standardization of some field material (irrigation and row cover). Ultimately, standardizing lets you keep your farm plan, with its smaller, digestible pieces, in your head.

FIELD LAYOUT TERMS

Field dimensions will vary depending on the machinery you use. A layout designed for walking tractors will be more compact than one designed for tractors.

Field Blocks

A field block is the basic unit in your field layout. All field blocks should contain an equal area of growing space. Ideally, all your field blocks should have the same number of beds of identical length.

Consider a field block a unit in your crop rotation; the beds that make up a block will be worked in a similar fashion. The actual dimensions of your field blocks will depend on the size and scale of your operation, as well as on the physical or geographical boundaries of your site.

Bed Width

Bed width is measured from the center of one path to the center of the next path.

Tractors need a bed width equal to the distance from the center of one tractor wheel to the center of the next, generally 1.5 or 1.8 m (60" or 72"). All your tractor equipment's wheels should have the same spacing or they will crush crops in adjacent beds. A bed width of 1.2–1.5 meters (48–60 inches) is adequate for walking tractors.

Bed Length

The choice of bed length is determined by your site and by your farming practices. Operating a tractor in short beds wastes time, since you frequently have to turn your machinery around in the headlands. Manually weeding long rows can be overwhelming because of the sheer size of the rows you have to weed or harvest. Tractor beds shouldn't be much shorter than 90 m (300 feet); a bed length of 30 m (100 feet) is adequate for walking tractors.

Number of rows per bed

Different vegetables tolerate different degrees of density on the bed. However, most growers standardize their field equipment to 3 rows per bed. This leaves the option to plant:

- All three rows
- The two outer rows
- Only the middle row

Row Spacing:

The space between rows and between plants within a row (inrow spacing) depends on your weeding tools.

- **Between-row spacing**
  - » Most weeding tools only need 30–45 cm (12–18") between rows to manoeuvre comfortably. Some crops (such as radishes or salad greens) can be planted more densely than this, though this may limit your weeding options to hand weeding.
- **Inrow spacing**
  - » Hand weeding: A spacing of 25–30 cm (10–12") will be most comfortable for hand tools.
  - » Tractor: A spacing of 25–30 cm (10–12") is necessary if you use tools that move in and out of the row. When implements bury inrow weeds, inrow spacing can be closer.

Non-growing space

The space around your blocks is made up of buffer zones, headlands, and access roads.

- **Buffer zones** are areas that separate your crops from neighbouring crops where pesticides, fertilisers or genetically modified seeds are used. The minimum width set by the Canadian Organic Standards is 8 meters (26 feet).

- **Headlands** refer to the area needed to turn your equipment around at the end of a bed. A headland of 8 to 12 m (26–40 ft) is adequate for most market garden scale tractors and implements.
- **Access roads** run parallel and perpendicular to your beds. They provide access to the middle of a field block without having to walk across your beds. They should be wide enough to accommodate a tractor. Access roads should give you access to any spot in your block without having to travel more than 30 m (100 ft).

FIELD LAYOUT RECOMMENDATIONS FOR DIFFERENT MECHANISATION LEVELS

	WALKING TRACTOR	RIDING TRACTOR
Bed Width	1.2 – 1.5 m (4 – 5 ft)	1.5 – 1.8 m (5 – 6 ft)
Bed Length	30 m (100 ft)	90 m (300 ft)
Distance between rows	0.3 – 0.45 m (12 – 18")	0.3 – 0.45 m (12 – 18")
Inrow Spacing	0.2 – 0.3 m (8 – 12")	0.2 – 0.3 m (8 – 12") for hand tools Closer for tractor cultivation
Headlands	3 – 8 m (10 – 26 ft)	8 – 10 m (26 – 33 ft)
Certification buffer zones	8 m (26 ft)	8 m (26 ft)

DESIGN FIELD BLOCKS

The fields at Tourne-Sol cooperative farm are divided into 17 half-acre blocks. Each block contains 14 beds, each 5 ft wide and 300 ft long.

At "Les Jardins de la Grelinette" 1.5 acres are divided into 10 blocks of 16 beds. Each bed is 4 feet wide by 100 ft long.

Draw sketches of all your different fields. Insert their dimensions. For each of your fields:

Define actual growing space

- Trim your field sketch to a rectangular area by removing perimeter non-growing areas (buffer zones, headlands, access paths).

Break growing space up into blocks

- Consider whether the width or length of your rectangular growing area would be a good bed length. Also consider whether the width or length might fit a multiple of your desired bed length (plus headlands).

- Divide your rectangular growing area into multiple rectangles (blocks) of the same size separated by headlands.
- Divide the width of these rectangles by your chosen bed width to determine how many beds wide the rectangles are.
- Aim to create between 5 to 20 blocks with 10 to 20 beds each.
- If the rectangles you create have different bed lengths, you can standardize your blocks to a given total area. Add the length of all the beds in your block to obtain the total bed length, and make sure all your blocks add up to the same total bed length.
- Puzzle out the basic block size that best accommodates your farming practices and your land. Every site is different. You don't always have to run beds and blocks in the same direction.

Make sure you have adequate access to the middle of your field blocks. Add access paths where needed. If space is too tight for dedicated paths, consider straddling empty beds (plan accordingly), or running over cover crops with your tractor or trucks (keep soil compaction in mind).

If you have more than 8 potential blocks and are having a hard time fitting them in the same area, consider having two sets of blocks. Each set can have its own rotation, irrigation equipment, and row cover.

As you create rectangular blocks in irregularly-shaped fields, you'll be left with odd-shaped nooks and corners. These potentially large areas can be used as additional growing space for flowers, herbs, seed production, perennials, fruit trees, or special trials that do not fit in your main annual crop plan. Be careful where you place perennial crops; they require a longer time commitment. In any case, it's more important to concentrate on carefully managing your field crop in the main field blocks.

Bruce and Hanna will plant 2 fields: one is roughly rectangular; the other is trapezoidal.

For their rectangular field A:
- *They measure 8 m (26 ft) from every edge to create a buffer zone. It should also be adequate as a headland for any tractors that might do custom work on their farm. This leaves a planting space of 65 m ✳ 47 m (213 ✳ 154 ft).*
- *They divide the 65 m (213 ft) length into two 30 m (100 ft) bed lengths and a 5 m (13 ft) headland. This headland is too tight for a tractor to turn, but it will accommodate a walking tractor.*

- *They divide the 47 m (154 ft)width into 1.5 m (5 ft) bed widths. This gives 31.3 beds. They settle on 30 beds.*
- *They decide on 15 beds per block. Each block has an area of 675 m² (15 * 1.5 m * 30 m) (approximately 7500 sq ft or 15 * 5 ft * 100 ft).*

For trapezoidal field B:
- *They measure 8 m (26 ft)from each edge to mark off non-growing space.*
- *They can easily fit one of their blocks in the growing space rectangle. This leaves an undefined rectangle of 17.5 m by 50 m (57 ft by 164 ft).*
- *They see if they can make a 675 m² (7500 sq ft) block with this rectangle.*
- *They divide 17.5 m (57 ft)width into 1.5 m (5 ft)beds. There is room for 11 beds. They decide to use 10 beds.*
- *They need a 45 m (150 ft)bed length*
  *[675 m² /(10 beds * 1.5 m) =45 m]*
  *(approximately: [7500 sqft/(10 beds * 5 ft)= 150 ft])*

Bruce and Hanna have 6 blocks. Each block is about 1/15th ha (1/6th acre). Blocks 1, 2, 3, 4 and 5 have 15 beds that are 30 m (100 ft)long and block 6 has 10 beds that are 45 m (150 ft)long. All their beds are 1.5 m (5 ft)wide.

BRUCE AND HANNA'S FINAL FIELD LAYOUT

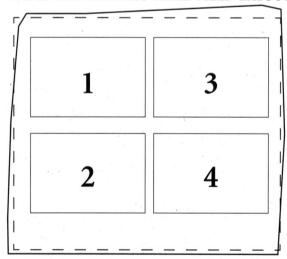
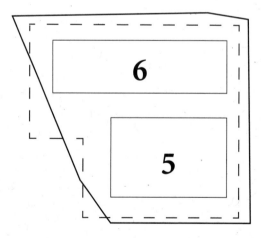

APPENDIX

C CROP PLANNING WITH SPREADSHEETS

CROP PLANNING can be done with paper and computers. Some great vegetable growers plan with both.

Computers are especially useful for copying information from one schedule to another, calculating total market sales, basket values, or bed lengths, and for setting dates.

If you would like to use a computer to crop plan and aren't familiar with spreadsheet software, there are only a handful of commands you will need to know:

- Embed formulas in a cell using the math operations: =, +, -, *, /, and ( )
- Use the summation operation
- Copy a formula from one cell to another by dragging it
- Change cell properties (format) to show the result of an equation as a date, currency, or a standard number

- Insert, copy and paste
- Manage appearance of cells, columns and rows
- Format the visual appearance of cells, text and borders
- Navigate from one worksheet to another
- Sort data on a worksheet

Here are a few examples of how computers can help you carry out the steps described in this book

STEP 2:
- Establish your price list and copy-paste it directly in your market needs, CSA basket content, and harvest needs worksheets.
- Compute total value of baskets and market sales in just a few clicks.

STEP 3:
- Use formulas to fill in planting weeks in crop worksheet, calculate planting dates, and figure out bed lengths to plant.
- Sort crops by families and quickly add total bed length for all the different crops in your preliminary planting schedule.

STEP 4:
- Balance block planting schedule and quickly see if actual bed length equals planned bed length.

D METRIC CHARTS

The tables presented throughout the text are in imperial units. This appendix presents the same tables in metric units.

TABLE 2.1 WEEKLY CSA SHARE CONTENT

CROP	$ VALUE	UNIT	02-JUL	09-JUL	16-JUL	23-JUL	30-JUL	06-AUG	13-AUG	20-AUG
Arugula	$2.50	bunch	1	1						
Basil	$2.50	bunch			1			1		
Beans	$6.00	kg			1	1	0.5	0.5	0.5	0.5
Beets	$2.50	bunch			1	1	1			1
Broccoli	$2.50	head	1	1	1	1	1	1	1	
Carrots	$2.50	bunch			1	1	1	1	1	1
Cilantro	$2.00	bunch	1			1				
Cucumbers	$0.75	fruit				3	3	3	3	3
Garlic	$1.50	head					1	1	1	
Kale	$2.50	bunch	1	1						
Kohlrabi	$1.50	head	2	1	1					
Lettuce	$2.00	head	1	1	1	1	1	1	1	1
Onions	$3.00	kg				1	1	1	1	1
Parsley	$2.00	bunch			1		1			1
Peas	$11.00	kg	1	1						
Peppers	$1.00	fruit							2	2
Potatoes	$3.00	kg								
Radish	$2.00	bunch	1	1	1					
Scallions	$2.00	bunch	1	1	1	1				
Squash, summer	$0.75	fruit				3	3	3	3	3
Tomatoes	$4.00	kg						1	1	1
WEEKLY SHARE VALUE IN $			$23.50	$24.50	$25.75	$24.50	$23.50	$25.50	$25.00	$25.50

CROP	27-AUG	03-SEP	10-SEP	17-SEP	24-SEP	01-OCT	08-OCT	15-OCT	TOTAL UNITS
Arugula					1	1	1		5
Basil	1			1					4
Beans	0.5	0.5	0.5	0.5					6
Beets	1	1				1	1	1	9
Broccoli					1	1	1	1	11
Carrots	1	1	1	1	1	1	1	1	14
Cilantro		1			1		1		5
Cucumbers	3	3	3						24
Garlic	1		1	2	2	2		2	13
Kale						1	1	1	6
Kohlrabi					1	1	1		7
Lettuce	1	1	1	1	1	1	1	1	16
Onions			1	1	1	1	1	1	11
Parsley		1				1		1	6
Peas									2
Peppers	2	2	2	2					12
Potatoes		1		1	1		1	1	5
Radish									3
Scallions									4
Squash, summer	3	3	3						27
Tomatoes	1	1	1	1					7
	$24.50	$25.50	$25.50	$25.00	$25.50	$25.50	$25.50	$23.00	

TABLE 2.2 WEEKLY MARKET SALES

CROP	$ VALUE	UNIT	02-JUL	09-JUL	16-JUL	23-JUL	30-JUL	06-AUG	13-AUG	20-AUG
Arugula	$ 2.50	bunch	15	15	15	15	15	15	15	15
Basil	$ 2.50	bunch			10	10	10	10	10	10
Beans	$ 6.00	kg								
Beets	$ 2.50	bunch		20	20	20	20	20	20	20
Broccoli	$ 2.50	head								
Carrots	$ 2.50	bunch			40	40	40	40	40	40
Cilantro	$ 2.00	bunch	15	15	15	15	15	15	15	15
Cucumbers	$ 0.75	fruit				75	75	75	75	75
Garlic	$ 1.50	head					50	50	50	50
Kale	$ 2.50	bunch	10	10	10	10	10	10	10	10
Kohlrabi	$ 1.50	head	15	15	15	15	15	15	15	15
Lettuce	$ 2.00	head	40	40	40	40	40	40	40	40
Onions	$ 3.00	kg				20	20	20	20	20
Parsley	$ 2.00	bunch		10	10	10	10	10	10	10
Peas	$ 11.00	kg	17.5	17.5						
Peppers	$ 1.00	fruit					30	30	30	30
Potatoes	$ 3.00	kg								
Radish	$ 2.00	bunch	20	20	20					
Scallions	$ 2.00	bunch	15	15	15	15				
Squash, summer	$ 0.75	fruit			60	60	60	60	60	60
Tomatoes	$ 4.00	kg						40	40	40
TARGET WEEKLY SALES IN $			$458	$528	$505	$581	$656	$816	$816	$816

Crop	27-AUG	03-SEPT	10-SEPT	17-SEPT	24-SEPT	01-OCT	08-OCT	15-OCT	22-OCT	TOTAL UNITS	TOTAL $
Arugula	15	15	15	15	15	15	15	15		240	$600
Basil	10	10	10	10						100	$250
Beans										0	$0
Beets	20	20	20	20	20	20	20	20	20	320	$800
Broccoli										0	$0
Carrots	40	40	40	40	40	40	40	40	40	600	$1,500
Cilantro	15	15	15	15	15	15	15	15	15	255	$510
Cucumbers	75	75	75	75	75					750	$563
Garlic	50	50	50	50	50	50	50	50	50	650	$975
Kale	10	10	10	10	10	10	10	10	10	170	$425
Kohlrabi	15	15	15	15	15	15	15	15	15	255	$383
Lettuce	40	40	40	40	40	40	40	40		640	$1,280
Onions	20	20	20	20	20	20	20	20	20	280	$840
Parsley	10	10	10	10	10	10	10	10	10	160	$320
Peas										35	$385
Peppers	30	30	30	30						240	$240
Potatoes										0	$0
Radish						20	20	20	20	140	$280
Scallions										60	$120
Squash, summer	60	60	60	60	60					660	$495
Tomatoes	40	40	40	40	40					320	$1,280
	$816	$816	$816	$816	$761	$540	$540	$540	$423		$11,245

TABLE 2.3 WEEKLY HARVEST TARGETS

CROP	UNIT	02-JUL	09-JUL	16-JUL	23-JUL	30-JUL	06-AUG	13-AUG	20-AUG	27-AUG	03-SEP	10-SEP	17-SEP	24-SEP	01-OCT	08-OCT	15-OCT	22-OCT	TOTAL UNITS
Arugula	bunch	50	50	15	15	15	15	15	15	15	15	15	15	50	50	50	15	0	415
Basil	bunch	0	0	45	10	10	45	10	10	45	10	10	45	0	0	0	0	0	240
Beans	kg	0	0	35	35	18	18	18	18	18	18	18	18	0	0	0	0	0	210
Beets	bunch	0	55	55	20	55	20	20	55	55	55	20	20	20	55	55	55	20	635
Broccoli	head	35	35	35	35	35	35	35	0	0	0	0	0	35	35	35	35	0	385
Carrots	bunch	0	0	75	75	75	75	75	75	75	75	75	75	75	75	75	75	40	1090
Cilantro	bunch	50	15	15	50	15	15	15	15	15	50	15	15	50	15	50	15	15	430
Cucumbers	fruit	0	0	0	180	180	180	180	180	180	180	180	180	75	75	0	0	0	1590
Garlic	head	0	0	0	0	85	85	85	50	85	50	85	120	120	120	50	120	50	1105
Kale	bunch	45	45	10	10	10	10	10	10	10	10	10	10	45	45	45	45	10	380
Kohlrabi	head	85	50	50	15	15	15	15	15	15	15	15	15	50	50	50	15	15	500
Lettuce	head	75	75	75	75	75	75	75	75	75	75	75	75	75	75	75	75	0	1200
Onions	kg	0	0	0	55	55	55	55	55	20	20	55	55	55	55	55	55	20	665
Parsley	bunch	0	45	10	10	45	10	10	45	10	10	45	10	10	45	10	45	10	370
Peas	kg	35	35	0	0	0	0	0	0	0	0	0	0	0	0	0	0	0	70
Peppers	fruit	0	0	0	0	30	30	100	100	100	100	100	100	0	0	0	0	0	660
Potatoes	kg	0	0	0	0	0	0	0	0	0	35	0	35	35	0	35	35	0	175
Radish	bunch	55	55	55	0	0	0	0	0	0	0	0	0	0	20	20	20	20	245
Scallions	bunch	50	50	50	50	0	0	0	0	0	0	0	0	0	0	0	0	0	200
Squash, summer	fruit	0	0	165	165	165	165	165	165	165	165	165	60	60	0	0	0	0	1605
Tomatoes	kg	0	0	0	0	0	75	75	75	75	75	75	75	40	0	0	0	0	565

Table 3.1 Bruce and Hanna's lettuce field worksheet

HARVEST DATE	DTM	FIELD DATE			HARVEST NEED HEADS	YIELD	ROWS PER BED	FIELD SF	BED LENGTH		
		CALCULATE FIELD DATE	ACTUAL FIELD DATE						CALCULATE PER WEEK	CALCULATE PER PLANTING	ACTUAL PER PLANTING
					HEADS	HEADS PER M			BEDM	BEDM	BEDM
03-JUL	35	29-MAY	22-MAY		75	3	3	1.3	9.85	9.85	10
10-JUL	35	05-JUN	05-JUN		75	3	3	1.3	9.85	19.7	20
17-JUL	35	12-JUN			75	3	3	1.3	9.85		
24-JUL	35	19-JUN	19-JUN		75	3	3	1.3	9.85	9.85	10
31-JUL	35	26-JUN			75	3	3	1.3	9.85	9.85	10
07-AUG	35	03-JUL	03-JUL		75	3	3	1.3	9.85	9.85	10
14-AUG	35	10-JUL	10-JUL		75	3	3	1.3	9.85	9.85	10
21-AUG	35	17-JUL	17-JUL		75	3	3	1.3	9.85	9.85	10
28-AUG	35	24-JUL	24-JUL		75	3	3	1.3	9.85	9.85	10
4-SEP	35	31-JUL	31-JUL		75	3	3	1.3	9.85	19.7	20
11-SEP	35	07-AUG			75	3	3	1.3	9.85		
18-SEP	35	14-AUG	14-AUG		75	3	3	1.3	9.85	49.24	50
25-SEP	35	21-AUG			75	3	3	1.3	9.85		
02-OCT	35	28-AUG			75	3	3	1.3	9.85		
09-OCT	35	04-SEP			75	3	3	1.3	9.85		
16-OCT	35	11-SEP			75	3	3	1.3	9.85		
23-OCT	35	18-SEP			0	3	3	1.3	0		

TABLE 3.2 PRELIMINARY FIELD PLANTING SCHEDULE

CROP	FAMILY	ROWS PER BED	INROW SPACING	FIELD PLANTING DATE					
				01-MAY	08-MAY	22-MAY	05-JUN	19-JUN	26-JUN
Garlic	Allium	3	0.15 m						
Onions	Allium	3	0.3 m		120				
Scallions	Allium	3	0.15 m		15				
Arugula	Brassica	3	DS			15		5	
Broccoli	Brassica	3	0.3 m		20	20	20	20	
Kale	Brassica	3	0.3 m			10		5	
Kohlrabi	Brassica	3	0.3 m			20		10	
Radish	Brassica	3	DS			15		10	
Lettuce	Aster	3	0.3 m			10	20	10	10
Beets	Chenopod	3	DS		40		40		
Basil	Labiatea	3	0.3 m			7.5	7.5	5	
Beans	Legumes	2	DS			60	30	30	
Peas	Legumes	1	DS	150					
Carrots	Umbel	3	DS		40		80		
Cilantro	Umbel	3	DS			7.5	5	10	
Parsley	Umbel	3	0.3 m		10		10		
Cucumbers	Cucurbits	1	DS			60		60	
Squash, summer	Cucurbits	1	DS			30		30	
Peppers	Solanacea	2	0.45 m				60		
Potatoes	Solanacea	1	DS			60			
Tomatoes	Solanacea	1	0.45 m				210		
						ALL BED LENGTHS IN BEDM			

			FIELD PLANTING DATE						TOTAL BED LENGTH	STAN-DARD BED LENGTH	TOTAL BEDS
03-JUL	10-JUL	17-JUL	24-JUL	31-JUL	14-AUG	28-AUG	11-SEP	16-OCT			
								90	90	30	3
									120	30	4
									15	30	0.5
5		5		5	5	15	10		65	30	2.2
			40						120	30	4
		5			15				35	30	1.2
10		10		10	30				90	30	3
						15			40	30	1.3
10	10	10	10	20	50				150	30	5
30		40		30					180	30	6
7.5		7.5							35	30	1.2
30		30							180	30	6
									150	30	5
80				100					300	30	10
5		5		10	15				58	30	2
15									35	30	1.2
		30							150	30	5
		30							90	30	3
									60	30	2
									60	30	2
									210	30	7
ALL BED LENGTHS IN BEDM											

Table 4.1 preliminary block planting schedule

Crop													TOTAL BED LENGTH	STANDARD BED LENGTH	TOTAL FULL BEDS
	01-MAY	08-MAY	22-MAY	05-JUN	19-JUN	26-JUN	03-JUL	10-JUL	17-JUL	24-JUL	31-JUL	14-AUG			
Lettuce			10	20	10	10	10	10	10	10	20	50	160	30	5.3
Beets		40		40			30		40		30		180	30	6
Basil			7.5	7.5	5		7.5		7.5				35	30	1.2
Beans			60	30	30		30		30				180	30	6
Peas	150												150	30	5
Carrots		40		80			80				100		300	30	10
TOTAL Bed length	150	80	78	178	45	10	158	10	88	10	150	50	1005	30	34
Target bed length	150	90	90	180	50	10	170	10	90	10	140	60	1050	30	
Target full beds	5	3	3	6	1.7	0.3	5.7	0.3	3	0.3	4.7	2			35

ALL BED LENGTHS IN BEDM

Table 4.2 balanced block planting schedule

Crop													TOTAL BED LENGTH	STANDARD BED LENGTH	TOTAL FULL BEDS
	01-MAY	08-MAY	22-MAY	05-JUN	19-JUN	26-JUN	03-JUL	10-JUL	17-JUL	24-JUL	31-JUL	14-AUG			
Lettuce			10	20	10	10	10	10	10	10	20	60	170	30	5.7
Beets		45		40			35		40		30		190	30	6.3
Basil			10	10	10		5		10				45	30	1.5
Beans			70	30	30		30		30				190	30	6.3
Peas	150												150	30	5
Carrots		45		80			90				90		305	30	10
TOTAL Bed length	150	90	90	180	50	10	170	10	90	10	140	60	1050	30	35

ALL BED LENGTHS IN BEDM

TABLE 4.3A CROP MAP FOR BLOCK OF EARLY MIXED CROPS

BED	CROPS			
1*	01-May Peas	31-July	Carrots *	
2*	01-May Peas	31-July	Carrots*	
3*	01-May Peas	31-July	Carrots *	
4*	01-May Peas	14-Aug	Lettuce *	
5*	01-May Peas	14-Aug	Lettuce *	
6	08-May Beets			
7	08-May 15 m Beets	15 m Carrots		
8	08-May Carrots			
9	22-May Beans			
10	22-May Beans			
11	22-May 10 m Lettuce	10 m Basil	10 m Beans	
12	05-Jun 20 m Lettuce	10 m Beets		
13	05-Jun Beets			
14	05-Jun Beans			
15	05-Jun 20 m Carrots	10 m Basil		

*Beds marked * are cropped a second time after first crop is finished.*

TABLE 4.3B CROP MAP FOR BLOCK OF LATE MIXED CROPS

BED	CROPS			
1	05-Jun Carrots			
2	05-Jun Carrots			
3	19-Jun Bean			
4	19-Jun 10 m Basil	10 m Lettuce	26-Jun	10 m Lettuce
5	03-Jul Beans			
6	03-Jul Beets			
7	03-Jul Carrots			
8	03-Jul Carrots			
9	03-Jul Carrots			
10	03-Jul 10 m Lettuce 10 m Basil	10-Jul	10 m Lettuce	
11	17-Jul Beans			
12	17-Jul Beets			
13	17-Jul 10 m Lettuce 10 m Beet	10 m Basil		
14	24-Jul 10 m Lettuce	31-Jul	20 m Lettuce	
15	31-Jul Beets			

TABLE 5.1A PORTION OF BRUCE AND HANNA'S FINAL FIELD PLANTING SCHEDULE

Crop	NOTES	FIELD PLANTING DATE												TOTAL BED LENGTH
		08-MAY	22-MAY	29-MAY	05-JUN	19-JUN	26-JUN	03-JUL	10-JUL	17-JUL	24-JUL	31-JUL	14-AUG	
LETTUCE			10		20	10	10	10	10	10	10	20	60	
Black Seeded Simpson	45 DTM				5	2.5	2.5	2.5	2.5	2.5	2.5	5	10	35
Salad Bowl	50 DTM				5	2.5	2.5	2.5	2.5	2.5	2.5	5		25
Red Oak	60 DTM		5		5	2.5	2.5	2.5	2.5	2.5	2.5	5	30	60
Jericho	57 DTM		5		5	2.5	2.5	2.5	2.5	2.5	2.5			25
Winter Density	55 DTM											5	20	25
BEETS		45			40			35		40		30		
Early Wonder		15			10			5		10				40
Detroit		15			15			15		15		15		75
Red Ace F1		15			15			15		15		15		75
TOMATOES				210										
Big Beef F1				60										60
New Girl F1				60										60
First Lady F1				60										60
Cherokee Purple				15										15
Green Zebra				15										15
ALL BED LENGTHS IN BEDM														

TABLE 6.1A PARTIAL LETTUCE GREENHOUSE WORKSHEET

								TRAYS TO SEED		
1	2	3	4	5	6	7	8	9	10	11
VARIETY	FIELD DATE	GH DAYS	GH DATE	BED LENGTH	ROWS PER BED	INROW SPACING	GH SF	TRAY SIZE	CALCULATE TRAYS	ACTUAL TRAYS
				BEDM		M				
Black Seeded Simpson	05-JUN	28	08-MAY	5	3	0.3	1.3	72	0.9	1
Salad Bowl	05-JUN	28	08-MAY	5	3	0.3	1.3	72	0.9	1
Red Oak	05-JUN	28	08-MAY	5	3	0.3	1.3	72	0.9	1
Jericho	05-JUN	28	08-MAY	5	3	0.3	1.3	72	0.9	1
Black Seeded Simpson	19-JUN	28	22-MAY	2.5	3	0.3	1.3	72	0.45	0.5
Salad Bowl	19-JUN	28	22-MAY	2.5	3	0.3	1.3	72	0.45	0.5
Red Oak	19-JUN	28	22-MAY	2.5	3	0.3	1.3	72	0.45	0.5
Jericho	19-JUN	28	22-MAY	2.5	3	0.3	1.3	72	0.45	0.5

TABLE 6.1B TOMATO GREENHOUSE WORKSHEET

								TRAYS TO PU				TRAYS TO SEED		
1	2	3	4	5	6	7	8	9	10	11	12	13	14	15
VARIETY	FIELD DATE	GH DAYS	GH DATE	BED LENGTH	ROWS PERBED	INROW SPACING	GH SF	TRAY SIZE	CALCULATE TRAYS	ACTUAL TRAYS	GH SF	SEEDED TRAY SIZE	CALCULATE TRAYS	ACTUAL TRAYS
				BEDM		M								
Big Beef	29-MAY	42	17-APR	60	1	0.45	1.1	50	2.93	3	1.3	98	1.99	2
New Girl	29-MAY	42	17-APR	60	1	0.45	1.1	50	1.99	3	1.3	98	1.99	2
First Lady	29-MAY	42	17-APR	60	1	0.45	1.1	50	1.99	3	1.3	98	1.99	2
Cherokee Purple	29-MAY	42	17-APR	15	1	0.45	1.1	50	0.66	1	1.3	98	0.66	0.7
Green Zebra	29-MAY	42	17-APR	15	1	0.45	1.1	50	0.33	0.5	1.3	98	0.33	0.3

Table 6.3 bruce and hanna's PARTIAL GH PLANTING SCHEDULE

| CROP | VARIETY | TRAY SIZE | SEEDS PER CELL | GH PLANTING DATE | | | | | | | | | | TOTAL SEEDED TRAYS | PU TRAYS | PU TRAY SIZE |
				24-APR	08-MAY	22-MAY	29-MAY	05-JUN	12-JUN	19-JUN	26-JUN	03-JUL	17-JUL			
Lettuce	Black Seeded Simpson	72	3		1	0.5	0.5	0.5	0.5	0.5	0.5	1	2	7		
Lettuce	Salad Bowl	72	3		1	0.5	0.5	0.5	0.5	0.5	0.5	1		5		
Lettuce	Red Oak	72	3	1	1	0.5	0.5	0.5	0.5	0.5	0.5	1	5.5	11.5		
Lettuce	Jericho	72	3	1	1	0.5	0.5	0.5	0.5	0.5	0.5			5		
Lettuce	Winter Density	72	3									1	3.5	4.5		
TOTAL TRAYS				2	4	2	2	2	2	2	2	4	11	33		
Tomato	Big Beef F1	98	1	2										2	3	50
Tomato	New Girl F1	98	1	2										2	3	50
Tomato	First Lady F1	98	1	2										2	3	50
Tomato	Cherokee Purple	98	1	0.7										0.7	1	50
Tomato	Green Zebra	98	1	0.3										0.3	0.5	50
TOTAL TRAYS				7	0	0	0	0	0	0	0	0	0	7	10.5	

TABLE 7.1 PARTIAL SEED WORKSHEET

CROP VARIETY	FOR DS	BED LENGTH (BEDM)	ROWS PER BED	SEED RATE	SEED SF	SEED COUNT	SEEDS PER GRAM	GRAMS	OUNCES	POUNDS
	FOR TP	TRAYS SEEDED	TRAY SIZE	SEEDS PER CELL						
BEETS										
Early Wonder	DS	40	3	50	1.3	7800	55	141.82	5.06	0.32
Detroit	DS	75	3	50	1.3	14625	55	265.91	9.5	0.59
Red Ace F1	DS	75	3	50	1.3	14625	55	265.91	9.5	0.59
TOMATOES										
Big Beef F1	TP	2	98	1	1.3	255	350	0.73	0.03	
New Girl F1	TP	2	98	1	1.3	255	350	0.73	0.03	
First Lady F1	TP	2	98	1	1.3	255	350	0.73	0.03	
Cherokee Purple	TP	0.7	98	1	1.3	89	350	0.25	0.01	
Green Zebra	TP	0.3	98	1	1.3	38	350	0.11	0.00	
LETTUCE										
Black Seeded Simpson	TP	7	72	3	1.3	1966	800	2.46	0.09	0.01
Salad Bowl	TP	5	72	3	1.3	1404	800	1.76	0.06	
Red Oak	TP	11.5	72	3	1.3	3229	800	4.04	0.14	0.01
Jericho	TP	5	72	3	1.3	1404	800	1.76	0.06	
Winter Density	TP	4.5	72	3	1.3	1264	800	1.58	0.06	

TABLE 7.2 BRUCE AND HANNA'S PARTIAL SEED ORDER

CROP VARIETY	SEED CATALOGUE	ITEM NUMBER	ORGANIC	QTY	FORMAT	$CAN	$US	TOTAL $CAN
BEETS								
Early Wonder				1	150 g			0
Detroit				1	300 g			0
Red Ace F1				15	300 g			0
TOMATOES								
Big Beef F1				1	1 g			0
New Girl F1				1	1 g			0
First Lady F1				1	1 g			0
Cherokee Purple				1	0.25 g			0
Green Zebra				1	0.25 g			0
LETTUCE								
Black Seeded Simpson				1	5 g			0
Salad Bowl				1	2 g			0
Red Oak				1	5 g			0
Jericho				1	2 g			0
Winter Density				1	2 g			0

E BRUCE AND HANNA'S DETAILED BUDGET

BRUCE AND HANNA'S BUDGET FOR THE FIRST YEAR

	$	%
INCOME	**22,000**	**100%**
Farmers Market	10,000	
CSA Baskets	12,000	
EXPENSES	**10,835**	**49%**
Fixed Costs		
ADMINISTRATION	1,490	7%
Bank Fees	240	
Computer material, Website	200	
Conferences	100	
Memberships (union, groups, etc.)	100	
Organic Certification	500	
Office supplies	150	
Professional fees (accountant, agronomist, etc.)	200	
INSURANCE	500	2%
Liability insurance	500	
LAND AND BUILDINGS	1,900	9%
Infrastructure maintenance	400	
Rent/business portion of mortgage	1,500	
FINANCIAL AND OTHER	1,270	6%
Depreciation	780	
Interest on loans	390	
Taxes	100	

	$	%
Operation Expenses		
SUPPLIES	1,650	8%
Fertilizers and amendments	250	
Irrigation	250	
Mulch	100	
Organic Pesticides	100	
Row Cover	250	
Seeds – Cover Crop	150	
Seeds – Crops	550	
GREENHOUSE	1,250	6%
Heating fuel or space rental	750	
Potting soil, containers, etc.	500	
FIELD OPERATIONS	725	3%
Contract work	300	
Fuel - Machinery	75	
Machinery Maintenance	100	
Small tools	250	
MARKETING	650	3%
Advertisement	100	
Market stall	300	
Packaging, harvest	250	
VEHICLE	800	4%
Mileage (fuel, repairs, registration, insurance)	800	
OTHER	600	3%
Farmer's Retained Earnings	**11,000**	**50%**
Profit	**165**	**1%**

FURTHER READING

CROP PLANNING

Kaplan, Dan. *Crop Planning Spreadsheets.* http://www.brookfieldfarm.org/cps.html

Rosenzweig, Marcie A. 1998. *Market Farm Forms.* Back 40 Books. (re-issued 2009, back-40books.com)

Crop planning software for small farmers and serious gardeners. http://code.google.com/p/cropplanning/

STEP 1 – SET YOUR FINANCIAL GOALS

Byczynski, Lynn. 2006. *Market Farming Success.* Fairplain Publications.

Equiterre. 2006. 4 *Modèles économiques viable et enviables d'ASC.* http://www.equiterre.org/agriculture/informer.php

Henderson, Elizabeth & North, Karl. 2004. *Whole Farm Planning: Ecological Imperatives, Personal Values and Economics.* Northeast Organic Farming Association Interstate Council.

Savory, Allan & Butterfield, Jody. 1999. *Holistic Management: A New Framework for Decision Making.* Island Press.

STEP 2 – MAKE A MARKETING PLAN

Bachman, Janet. 2004. *Selling to Restaurants: Business and Marketing.* ATTRA. www.attra.org

Gibson, Eric. 1994. *Sell What you Sow.* New World Publishing.

Growing For Market. 2009. *Special Report: Selling at Farmers Markets.* Fairplain Publications http://www.growingformarket.com/categories/20071227

Henderson, Elizabeth, and Van En, Robyn. 2007. *Sharing the Harvest, A Citizen's Guide to Community Supported Agriculture.* Chelsea Green Publishing.

Hunter, Elizabeth, 2000. *Je Cultive Tu Manges Nous Partageons.* Equiterre.

Ishee, Jeff. 1997. *Dynamic Farmers' Marketing.* Bittersweet Farmstead.

Steps 3 – 8 – the crop plan

GENERAL VEGETABLE GROWING

Brisebois, Daniel and Board, Emily. 2007. *Irrigation for small to medium-sized gardens*. The Canadian Organic Grower, Fall 2007.

Centre de référence en agriculture et agroalimentaire du Québec (CRAAQ). 2003. *Guide de référence en fertilisation, 1re edition*. Centre de référence en agriculture et agroalimentaire du Québec (CRAAQ)

Coleman, Eliot. 1995. *The New Organic Grower*. Chelsea Green Publishing

Gagnon, Yves. 2003. *La Culture Écologique Pour Petites et Grandes Surfaces*. 3ieme edition révisée. Les Éditions Colloïdales.

Gagnon, Yves. 2004. *La Culture Écologique Des Plantes Légumières*. 2ieme edition. Les Éditions Colloïdales.

Grubinger, Vernon. 1999. *Sustainable Vegetable Production from Start-Up to Market*. Natural, Resource, Agriculture, and Engineering Services (NRAES).

La France, Denis. 2007. *La Culture Biologique des Légumes*. Éditions Berger A.C.

Maynard, Donald N. and Hochmuth, George J. 1997. *Knotts Handbook for Vegetable Growers*. 4th ed. John Wiley & Sons, Inc.

Satzewich, Wally and Christensen, Roxanne. *SPIN-Farming learning guides*. http://www.spinfarming.com/

Solomon, Steve. 2005. *Gardening When it Counts*. New Society Publishers.

CROP ROTATION AND COVER CROPS:

Kroeck, Seth. 2005. *Soil Resiliency and Health: Crop Rotation and Cover Cropping on the Organic Farm*. Northeast Organic Farming Association Interstate Council.

Mohler, Charles and Johnson, Sue Ellen, eds. 2009. *Crop Rotation on Organic Farms: a Planning Manual*. Natural, Resource, Agriculture, and Engineering Services (NRAES).

Nordell, Anne and Eric. 2007. *Weed the Soil, Not the Crop: A Whole Farm Approach to Weed Management*. excerpt and ordering information at www.acresusa.com/toolbox/reprints/June09_Nordells.pdf

Northeast Organic Network (NEON). 2002. *Guide to the Expert Farmers' DACUM Chart for Manage Crop Rotation System*. http://www.neon.cornell.edu/croprotation/

Sarrantonio, Marianne. 1994. *Northeast Cover Crop Handbook*. Rodale Institute.

Sustainable Agriculture Network. 2007. *Managing Cover Crops Profitably*. www.sare.org/publications/index.htm

GREENHOUSE MANAGEMENT

Bubel, Nancy. 1988. *The New Seed-Starters Handbook*. Rodale Press.

OMAFRA. 1996. *Growing Vegetable Transplants In Plug Trays*. http://www.omafra.gov.on.ca/english/crops/facts/96-023.htm

CULTIVATION TOOLS

Sustainable Agriculture Network. 2002. *Steel in the Field*. www.sare.org/publications/index.htm

SEASON EXTENSION

Bycsynski, Lynn, ed. 2006. *The Hoophouse Handbook*. Fairplain Publications.

Coleman, Eliot. 2009. *The Winter Harvest Handbook*. Chelsea Green Publishing.

Grohsgal, Brett. 2004. *Time to get ready for winter*. Growing for Market Vol 13 # 8.

Grohsgal, Brett. 2004. *Winter Crops, Part 2: Planting Through Marketing*. Growing for Market Vol 13 # 9.

Grohsgal, Brett. 2007. *Innovation & Risk Management: The Yin and Yang of Farm Success*. Growing for Market Vol 16 # 7.

STEP 10 — ANALYZE CROP PROFITABILITY

Arnold, Paul and Sandy. 2004. *Profitability on a Small Farm*. Eco Farm & Garden Volume 7 Number 1.

Wiswall, Richard. 2009. *The Organic Farmer's Business Handbook*. Chelsea Green Publishing.